D0205720

WITHDRAWN

Outside Looking In

Outside Looking In

An African Perspective on American Pluralistic Society

Kofi K. Apraku

MAR 1 7 1998

Westport, Connecticut
London

Library of Congress Cataloging-in-Publication Data

Apraku, Kofi Konadu.
    Outside looking in : an African perspective on American
pluralistic society / Kofi K. Apraku.
        p.   cm.
    Includes bibliographical references.
    ISBN 0–275–94207–4 (alk. paper)
    1. United States—Social conditions—1980–   2. United States—
Politics and government—20th century. 3. United States—Ethnic
relations.   I. Title.
HN59.2.A58   1996
306′.0973—dc20   94–12349

British Library Cataloguing in Publication Data is available.

Copyright © 1996 by Kofi K. Apraku

All rights reserved. No portion of this book may be
reproduced, by any process or technique, without the
express written consent of the publisher.

Library of Congress Catalog Card Number: 94–12349
ISBN: 0–275–94207–4

First published in 1996

Praeger Publishers, 88 Post Road West, Westport, CT 06881
An imprint of Greenwood Publishing Group, Inc.

Printed in the United States of America

∞™

The paper used in this book complies with the
Permanent Paper Standard issued by the National
Information Standards Organization (Z39.48–1984).

10 9 8 7 6 5 4 3 2

Copyright Acknowledgments

The author and publisher gratefully acknowledge permission for use of the following material:

Excerpts from A. Adu Boahen, *African Perspectives on Colonialism* (Baltimore, MD: Johns Hopkins University Press, 1990).

Excerpts from Kevin P. Phillips, *Mediacracy* (New York: Doubleday, 1975). Copyright © 1975 Kevin P. Phillips.

For Helena, the children, my mother, the Robertsons,
and all aspiring African writers.

The Maze

by Angelina Adoquaye

Dry Season, Wet Season
Tell different tales
Each passing day, every passing night
Spring up indelible surprises
Honour thy father and mother! But
in His goodness, I am created as equal
Is Freedom at stake?
The flower is yet unbruised.

Life seems a macabre, through
Winter, Spring, Summer and Autumn
Am I my brother's keeper?
No one is a brother's keeper
Yet the Statue of Liberty still stands
The bruised rose flower
The Invisible cuddles it
The Visible touches it
Yes! Melting Pot keeps churning.

The steaming Crucible:
Black and White
Lawyers and Teachers
Vates and Clergymen
Politicians and Laymen
Boiling, Sizzling, Tossing, Rising
The result -- ripples
When the hurly-burly is done
After the Herculean task
Let's stand and ask
Is life ever going to be fair?

Contents

Preface

This book is a reflection of my over two decades experience and impressions about the United States. During this period, several people made significant impressions on me. My host family, the Jack Robertsons, provided the love and direction that sustained me during my early years in the United States as a high school exchange student in Albany, Oregon. They made a significant and profound impression on my fragile and impressionable mind. I have since then gained tremendously from my school and university classmates, from my professional colleagues, from friends, students and neighbors. Who I am, what I think, my attitudes, perceptions, and insights have greatly been influenced by these interactions.

This book is not an indictment of the United States; rather it is an appreciation of the United States. If it is any good at all, it will provide a different perspective, perhaps a new way to look at the problems that confront the nation. And if this is so, it may well be my way of saying thank you to the United States for being a home away from home to me for the past two decades.

Indeed, as I wrote this book, I could not help but reflect on what John F. Kennedy, then an aspiring president, said of the United States, "America is great but it can be greater." Yes, I also believe that the United States is great, but can be made greater. The sentiment thus expressed in this book is my contribution to the discussions and debates aimed at that objective. Furthermore, it is hoped that this book will enable Africans to appreciate the strengths and successes of the United States while avoiding its mistakes. Yet, I am painfully aware that a book such as this, with its generalizations about Africa and the United States and its frank discussions of the problems faced in both societies, will necessarily arouse controversy. I welcome this controversy with an open mind and hope it will generate healthy and objective discussions.

In this book, I have tried to limit the use of the name "America." In those instances where it is needed, it refers to the United States of America, and not the entire people of North America.

Several people have been supportive of my work, and I would like to pay tribute to a few here. My beloved family has not only been supportive of my professional and political activities, but they have also actively encouraged these activities. They have paid for these activities, especially my political adventures, with their personal comfort and security, and long periods of separation. I am forever indebted to them.

Parts of the manuscript were reviewed and commented on by friends, students, and colleagues. I greatly benefited from comments by Dr. Bill Sabo, chair of the Political Science Department at University of North Carolina-Asheville; Dr. Susan Kask, assistant professor of economics at Western Carolina University; and Michael England, a student in my Humanities class. I am similarly thankful to the following persons who reviewed parts of the manuscript and made suggestions for improvement; Angelina Adoquaye, Professor Adu Boahen, Dr. Pamela Nickless, Dr. Agyemang Gyawu, Dr. Stephen Kyereme, Dr. Don Locke, and Benjamin Duodu. Several of my students participated in various surveys I conducted in preparing the manuscript. To all these students I am greatly thankful.

The manuscript was delayed for more than one year when I ran for parliamentary office in Ghana. Greenwood Publishers was kind to extend the deadline and has since been both supportive and cooperative. I am thankful to them, especially to my acquisitions editor, Dr. James Ice, and production editor, Dr. Karen Davis. The camera-ready copy of this book was prepared by Sharon Pippert. I am very thankful to her. I am equally thankful to Sheri Brophy for her assistance in proofreading. Finally, I am thankful to the University of North Carolina at Asheville for its support.

Introduction

After what appeared to be an endless number of hours on the plane, we finally touched down at JFK International Airport in New York. The day was July 21, 1972, a beautiful summer day with clear blue skies. A dream had actually come true. The America I was beholding was more beautiful than any book could have described. The summer day was warm and beautiful with people briskly going about their business. The city was very alive, bouncing with activity. As we drove from the airport into the city, I could not help thinking about the crowded nature of the city. There were people all over, blacks and whites. I had never seen so many white people in my life. The noise of cars, buses, and people kept reminding me of a market scene in Ghana.

I had not expected to see so many people in constant motion like this in America. I had expected to see a more orderly movement of people who were well dressed and well mannered. The constant honking of horns by taxi drivers, careening recklessly by, again put my mind back to a scene on a busy Accra street or a busy Lagos street.

As the skyline of Manhattan came into view, it struck me for the first time that the United States may indeed be the ultimate land of opportunity and beauty. Even though, to my disappointment, I could not find any sidewalk paved with gold, I felt quite reassured that a new chapter in my life had begun. Everything seemed to be going well for me. The beautiful summer weather was an endorsement, even a good omen, of the great things to come. After all, my readings in preparation for this trip had me believing that nothing remains constant for long in the United States.

It had been mentioned to me that in a country where everything seems to be in extremes the summers could be uncomfortable, even for a person coming from a tropical zone. This was not to be the case, at least not today. I needed all the good fortune I could get on my first day in the United States. Had I not been told many times by my mother that if you start well you end well? So I was determined that everything would go well for me today. I was delighted and optimistic about the future.

I had also been told that the United States is the ultimate land of opportunity, that the limit to one's achievement is set only by one's own imagination, and that a determined person can literally reach for the stars. As if to reassure myself, I murmured to myself, "Didn't America literally reach for the stars when it landed man on the moon? Sure, everything is possible in this country."

The trip from the airport to C.W. Post University in Long Island, where I was to spend three days for orientation, seemed to take forever. I was excited and very impatient to end this trip. It seemed like I had been in constant motion for months. I wished very much that this seemingly never-ending journey would come to an end. The trip was becoming quite unbearable.

I needed something to occupy my mind. The sight of many black people in the city instantly provided an appropriate focus of attention for me. I was first surprised to see so many black people in the city. In preparation for this trip, I had read about the sufferings and the plight of the black Americans in the United States. Somehow, a lot of Africans feel a sense of responsibility for the part that our ancestors played in the enslavement of black Americans in the United States and elsewhere. I have always wondered why they would not return to Africa if indeed they were being mistreated in the United States.

Suddenly, like Gatheru Mungo, I also felt a strong urge to get out of the car and talk to them, to identify with them, to tell them how much I knew about their plight in the United States and how much we in Africa support their cause, and generally to express my solidarity with people I considered my own kind.[1] Rather suddenly, I felt homesick, and I quickly reflected on Ghana. A strong sense of loss seemed to have taken over my recent optimism and excitement, and I felt very sad. For the first time in my life I felt like a minority; unknowingly, as I was to find out later, I had been transformed from a proud majority to a second-class minority.

I felt myself thinking about Ghana and contrasting it with the United States. The contrast was overwhelming and almost unbearable. A few hours ago, I had left behind one country for a new one. I found two countries with tremendous contrast. Behind me in Ghana, I had left a country devastated by an unexpected and unwarranted military coup d'etat that had overthrown the democratically elected government of Dr. Kofi Busia. A once dynamic and relatively prosperous country, the Ghana I left behind was on the verge of economic and political collapse.

When it became independent in 1957, Ghana was one of Britain's richest colonies in Africa. Ghana's constitution and its level of economic and political development were held up as examples of democracy for the rest of Africa. Ghana, the former Gold Coast, had become independent with much fanfare, goodwill, and a budget surplus of more than $400 million. It also had the advantage of dynamic leadership under Kwame Nkrumah, an extensive and well-developed educational system, and a physical infrastructure that could facilitate its rapid development.

The promise of rapid development was evident in the early years of independence when Ghana completed many important development projects, including the construction of the Tema harbor, the development of the Valco Aluminum processing plants, and further development of educational and other supporting infrastructures throughout the country. Despite its impressive start, prospects for any sustained growth were dashed in the early 1960s.

By 1963, for example, the budget surplus of the early postindependence era had been replaced by a large government budget deficit. The relative political and economic freedoms enjoyed by Ghanaians in the early years of independence were largely gone. With the economy teetering on the edge of collapse and political leadership becoming increasingly autocratic and repressive, the stage was set for Ghana's demise, which followed more quickly than most expected.

By the 1970s, military intervention and coup d'etat had become a common feature of Ghana's political life, and with that the economy sank aground. When I left my country in 1972, it was suffering both a political and an economic malaise that very few could have imagined at the time of independence.

Like many African countries, Ghana has become hostage to greedy, inefficient, corrupt, and undisciplined military and political institutions that are intent solely on gaining and holding power, even at the peril of the national interest. In many ways, Ghana is a microcosm of a continent gone wrong -- a continent where economic mismanagement, political corruption, tribalism, civil wars, and military coups have conspired against progress. Africa, the continent where humankind originated, seems to have lost its sense of direction, purpose, and, most importantly, control over its own destiny. The Ghana I had left behind a few hours ago, like the rest of Africa, appeared to have lost even the will to try.

The United States, on the other hand, seemed so full of life and hope, energy and purpose. The 1972 presidential campaign that pitted George McGovern against incumbent President Richard Nixon was well underway. The Vietnam War that had torn the country apart and appeared to have undermined the very fabric of the American society was also coming to an end. In general, there was a conspicuous air of hope and optimism that proved rather affective.

I tried without success to rid my mind of the situation in Ghana and to focus on the opportunities that lay ahead of me.

Everything had happened too fast. I never really thought I would ever come to the United States. Actually, I had no right even to expect that. Even though my father was relatively rich, he had not taken much interest in my education. First, because he and my mother were divorced, and second, being an illiterate himself, he had not taken much interest in education in general. As a result of these factors and the large financial requirement that it takes to travel abroad, the idea of coming to the United States, terrific as it may be, was nothing that I had given much thought to. Luckily, however, I did not have to be rich.

It all started when my English teacher urged me to enter a national essay competition that was organized under the auspices of the American Field Service (AFS) International Scholarship Exchange Program. Successful candidates in the competition are selected to represent Ghana in various high schools in the United States. I entered the competition very reluctantly for two reasons. First, I was quite aware that corruption and nepotism prevalent at that time in Ghana gave very little chance for an average person like myself without any important contacts, and second, all the previous participants in the exchange program had come from the elite schools in Ghana. My school obviously was not an elite school. Located only a few miles from Kumasi, the Asante capital, Tweneboa Kodua Secondary School had been named after Tweneboa Kodua, an Asante chief, who had a unique place in Asante history. During one of the toughest Asante wars, the chief priest of the Asantehene had demanded that a human sacrifice be made to the gods in order to ensure victory. The Asante history records that the Kumawuhene, Nana Tweneboa Kodua, offered himself as the sacrificial lamb so that the Asantes could win the war.

The Asantes won the war, and in recognition of his valor this school was built and named for him. Although this school has a rich history and was generally a good school, it was not one the top schools in the country. No student from my school had ever been selected to participate in the exchange program. These odds intensified my desire to succeed. Suddenly, I had developed a burning desire to be selected for the exchange program.

Having officially entered the competition, I devoted a great amount of my time to reading autobiographies of some of the world's most important people, all in preparation for the essay competition that was titled "my autobiography."

Nearly a year after submitting the essay, I was invited for an interview in Accra, the capital of Ghana. I had never been to Accra before. With the help of my brother, I managed to assemble a few decent clothes for the trip. After three rounds of rigorous interviews, I was quite sure that I had made a positive impression on the panel and could expect a positive recommendation.

About four weeks after the interview, my expectation was realized. I was notified that my interview had been successful and that I have been selected along with some twelve other Ghanaian youth to participate in the exchange program that year. I was also notified that I would be spending my year in the United States at South Albany High School in Albany, Oregon. My host family would be the Jack Robertsons. A few days later, I received a package from my host parents-to-be in which they included pictures of their entire family and a newspaper clipping of a story that had appeared in the local newspaper announcing my selection as the local AFS student and my enrollment at South Albany in the coming fall.

The Robertsons, a family of four, were a middle-income American family. My host mother was a school teacher, and my host father ran his own taxidermy business. My host sister was a freshman at Oregon State University, and my host brother, at my age, would be a senior with me at South Albany.

The next few months were devoted to preparing for the upcoming trip. I read every book I could lay my hands on about the United States and Oregon. As a potential "ambassador" for Ghana, I also learned as much as I could about Ghanaian culture, customs, habits, and foods. The AFS office in Ghana helped the exchange students greatly in this respect. The office organized tours that were aimed at familiarizing us with different parts of Ghana.

These tours were quite useful for me, in particular because I had not traveled much outside my own region of Ghana. We went to museums, cultural centers, sites of development projects, the Aburi gardens, educational institutions such as the University of Ghana, the Akosombo dam, and many other places of historic and national interest.

While it was necessary for us to learn as much as we could about Ghana before our departure for the United States, it was equally important that we learn just as much about the United States. The AFS program office in Ghana was determined to make our transition into American society as smooth as possible in order to reduce potential cultural shock. The AFS office accordingly planned an elaborate orientation program for us in Ghana.

As part of our orientation, they arranged for us to stay with American families (generally, American diplomats) for one week in Accra. This week of orientation was very useful in exposing us to American foods, culture, habits, and to the American way of life.

The orientation had an unanticipated effect on me. For the first time I came into direct contact with the elite society in Ghana. I had never before lived in a home with a swimming pool, air conditioner, washing machine, tennis court, and many other luxuries that were being enjoyed exclusively by the expatriate community and their elite Ghanaian counterparts. With my largely rural background, I did not even know that such a life-style was possible in a largely poor country.

This experience had a tremendous impact on me. I resolved to work hard in the United States to make something of myself not only so that I could live this kind of life, but also so that I could help improve the living conditions for the poor, especially those like myself, born and reared in the rural areas of Ghana, people whom I was now leaving behind. I felt a sense of responsibility to these people. I was determined to return to Ghana someday and make their cause my cause and to work to improve their lives. Exactly how I would do that was irrelevant -- so I thought, at least. I was, however, sure that someday "I shall return." For the time being, I was incapable of indulging in any details; my mind was set on America!

It all came together when on July 21, 1972, I arrived in New York's JFK airport on a Pan American chartered flight with about four hundred youth from 143 countries to begin a year of learning and fun in American schools and communities. After two days of orientation on the campus of C. W. Post University in Long Island, I flew to Portland, Oregon, where I was met by my host parents.

For the next ten years, I was determined to take America at its word -- it was the "land of opportunity where if you played fair you would be rewarded." During that period, I completed my last year in high school and won a state of Oregon scholarship to study at Oregon State University. I received my bachelor of science degree in 1977 and my master of science degree in 1979. In January 1980, I started my Ph.D. work at the Ohio State University and completed the degree in September 1983. That same month, I took my first professional job as an assistant professor of economics and finance at Rio Grande College in Ohio.

Since then, I have traveled extensively in the United States -- from north to south, from east to west. I have lived in four states, and taught at three colleges and universities. I have given more than a hundred speeches to groups and organizations. I have organized seminars and workshops, and chaired sessions at professional meetings. I have come to know something about America's strengths and weaknesses.

I have also learned that in many cases, America's greatest strengths and ideals -- freedom, liberty, hard work, individualism, achievement and success, and its competitive spirit -- are also the causes of America's greatest weaknesses -- crime, alcoholism and drugs, stress, depression, emotional instability, breakdown of the family, child abuse, apathy, greed, and corruption.

This book is an account of my experiences in the United States, and most importantly, my impressions and observations about the American society and people. This is a most difficult assignment because a story of the kind I intend to tell requires so many generalizations. But America does not lend itself to easy generalization, classification, or categorization. America is too complex for that. It is made up of perhaps the most heterogeneous groups of people in the world and cannot be explained away so easily.

I have always wondered, for example, how you can explain a nation where the government spends over $300 billion annually on national defense when more than 30 million of its 250 million citizens live below the national poverty line, and over 2 million of its citizens are homeless, living on the streets and eating from garbage cans. How do you explain a nation that claims to be the greatest civilization the world has ever known when in that same civilized nation, a serious crime is committed every 3.5 seconds, one robbery is reported every 83 seconds, and one murder is committed every 27 minutes?

How do you explain a great civilization where 2 to 4 million helpless children are abused and raped annually? How do you explain a country where there are half a million heroin addicts and over 9 million alcoholics?

How do you explain a country that professes to be the leader of the free world but has kept and continues to keep company with some of the world's most renowned brutal dictators, the likes of the Shah of Iran, Marcos of the Philippines, Samoza of Nicaragua, Botha of South Africa, Mobutu of Zaire, and Pinochet of Chile, to name only a few? How do you explain a society that preaches freedom and equality abroad but finds it unnecessary to ratify a constitutional amendment that will confer equality on women?

How do you explain a civilized nation that even today continues to judge people not by the content of their character but by the color of their of their skin?

Yet, behind every American failure, there is a great success story. America, for example, provides one of the highest standards of living for its citizens. It offers its citizens more economic, personal, social, and political freedoms than perhaps any country in the world. American generosity is known throughout the world. In 1991 it provided more than $17 billion in foreign aid (generally to serve its own economic, military, and security self-interest, but also for humanitarian purposes), more than any other country on the face of the earth.

The United States' achievement in science and technology, as well as in agriculture, has been one of its greatest contributions to humankind. The less than 3 percent of Americans who engage in agriculture feed the entire country and provide more than one-third of the world's food supply.

The assignment that is ahead of me in the next few chapters centers on the enormous contradictions in American society. There is no simple explanation for the American character, behavior, achievement, or for the American failures. Yes, America may not be a perfect country, but that is not for lack of trying.

This book is a personal account of more than twenty years in this country. It is intended to serve three main purposes. First, as an African, with years of experience in the United States, I have gained some valuable insights into the American culture, character, and life-style. As such, I feel an obligation to the world, and most importantly to Africa, to share my impressions and experiences in the United States. Africa today is under siege.

There is a violent clash of culture in Africa: the traditional culture against modern culture, and the African culture against the Western culture. The winner in this clash is obvious. Africans are abandoning everything African, and in its place they are installing Western cultures, values, life-styles, tastes, and preferences. Western music is preferred over African music. African art today is designed for Western consumers. Today Africa is uncertain about its identity, future, and purpose, and foreign influence is manifested in every corner of the large continent.

Where colonialism did not achieve total success, cultural imperialism has, and where cultural imperialism has not been successful, economic imperialism already reigns. Highly trained and educated Africans leave their responsible positions in Africa only to become taxi drivers in New York, Washington, D.C., and other American cities. The image of American streets paved with gold still lingers in many parts of Africa. Yes, America may be a land of opportunity, but this land of opportunity has its fair share of problems that Africans must know. The American story, to the extent that it affects Africans, must be told just as it is -- nothing more, nothing less.

My second reason for writing this book can best be explained with a short story. One day a little boy returned from school obviously upset. He charged straightforward to his dad and said, "Father, why have you been lying to me all these years?" With a mixture of anger, frustration, and love, the father responded, "What's the matter, son? I have never lied to you." The son shot back, "You lied to me when you told me that the lion is the king of the jungle. That's not true. If the lion is the king of the jungle why is it that every story that I have read or been told ends with the lion either being killed or defeated?" The father looked at his son affectionately, took him in his arms, and said, "Son, the story will always end like that until the lion learns to write, and writes his own story." As an African, I feel very much like the lion.

We Africans have been put down partly because we have had others write our story. As a people, our history has been written by others; our textbooks are written overseas; foreigners who are on a casual visit to Africa, or spend a few months in Africa, become instant authorities on Africa and soon propound theories about Africa that eventually become reference and historical documents.

Above all, the African story has been written from a Eurocentric perspective -- either by imperialist historians, colonial administrators, or anthropologists -- all with different interests and agendas. The real African story can only be written with African collaborators, and then, only then, can we change both the story and its ending. I hope this book will inspire other Africans, as I have been inspired by others, to write about their experiences and about their professions.

Again, as I have traveled around the United States, giving lectures, I have found that many Americans are interested in learning about Africa. Often, people have asked me, "What do you like most about the United States? What are the outstanding differences that you see between the people, customs, life-styles, foods, in the United States and Africa?" For these, and others, who are interested in learning about Africa and about how many Africans feel about the United States, this book will attempt to provide some answers.

Third, I believe that this book is timely. The world has experienced a tremendous euphoria following the so-called democratic revolutions that swept authoritarian communist governments in Eastern and Central Europe in the late 1980s. In the wake of these revolutions, Western democratic political institutions have been touted as the wave of the future, and small and large countries, poor and not-so-poor countries, from Asia to Latin America, Central to Eastern Europe, and Africa to the Caribbean, have been urged to get on board the democratic bandwagon before they lose their economic aid from the West.

Many people in these countries, including Africans, do not know enough about Western democracy or the American democratic system that they are being asked to adopt as a panacea to their economic, political, and social problems. The question that must be asked is, What are the strengths and weaknesses of the American brand of democratic political system that are most helpful to Africa?

This book provides an African perspective of the opportunities, but even more important, the challenges that face a pluralistic democratic country. It addresses critical weaknesses that are inherent in the American democratic system and society but many times have been ignored when Africans assessed American society and its institutions from afar. For example, are Africans fully aware of the demands of a democratic society? Would democracy necessarily cure Africa's enormous economic, social, ethnic, and political problems? Can democracy eliminate corruption, nepotism, cronyism, and incompetence, or does democracy exacerbate these problems?

In this critical period in Africa's history, I believe there is much that Africa can learn from the American experience. This account of my experience in the United States is my small contribution to this learning process.

Chapter 1 answers the question, "What makes the United States a great nation"? It discusses America's greatness -- its natural resources, agricultural abundance, and military, economic, and technological power. It examines what are generally considered to be American values and ideals and to be most responsible for America's greatness -- freedom, equality, liberty, hard work, thrift, individualism, competitive spirit, ingenuity, and social justice -- from both historical and modern perspectives. Finally, the chapter examines whether or not the expectations and dreams of recent immigrants to the United States match the realities of life in the United States.

Chapter 2 examines the price that the United States has paid for its material, economic, and technological successes. It is argued in this chapter that, ironically, the same values and ideals that make the United States a great nation also cause its great failings. The problems in the United States, it is thus argued, arise out of America's economic and material success, overemphasis on individualism, unrestrained freedoms, competitive and can-do spirit, and consuming desire for achievement and individual success. Having been responsible for the United States' successes, these same values and ideals are today contributing to the high crime rate, high incidence of alcoholism and drug dependency, high divorce rate, high incidence of stress-related health problems, and child abuse in the United States. It is also argued in this chapter that wallowing in their material and economic successes, Americans have become apathetic and ignorant about the world around them, including their own.

Chapter 3 discusses the American nuclear family and contrasts it with the African extended family. The chapter starts with a discussion of my family background in an African polygamous situation and its attendant problems. It records my earliest fascination with the American family which I had associated with understanding, love, affection, stability, individualism, equality, closeness, and tolerance. My disappointment with the American family came when the dark side of the American family -- the high divorce rate, infidelity, child abuse, illegitimate births, lack of discipline, teenage suicide, and teenage drug and alcohol abuse -- is revealed to me later in my stay in the United States. This state of affairs really breaks my heart.

Chapter 4 starts with a discussion of the democratization process that has been going on in Africa since the aftermath of the Cold War. Since the end of the Cold War, many African countries have embarked on democratization with the support of Western donor nations. Many donor countries have demanded that African countries undertake political reforms in order to continue to receive aid. The United States' political system has been offered as a successful democratic model for these countries. But most Africans do not know enough about the workings, strengths, and weaknesses of the United States' brand of democracy. This chapter examines the strengths and weaknesses of the American political system and its viability for Africa. It is argued that two of the major problems that face the American political system are low voter participation in the political system and the undue influence of the media on the political system. As voter participation in the political process has declined, the news media, and television in particular, have by default assumed the kingmaker role in American politics. In the process, politics in the United States has become a competition for images rather than for ideas.   American politics has become show business, the embodiment of this development being the election of Ronald Reagan as president in 1980.

In Chapter 5 the growing influence of interest group politics and the effect on the American democratic process are discussed. It is argued that one of the major effects of the news media on the political process is increasing election spending which has tended to confine political office to candidates who are either independently wealthy or willing to sell their soul to the proliferating political interest groups. After examining problems that plague the United States' political system, the question is raised as to whether or not the same problems that tend to be associated with politics in Africa -- political corruption, abuse of power, trust, and office, nepotism, crony politics -- are not commonplace in United State's politics.

Chapter 6 discusses my experiences in the United States as a black person. The disappointment I felt with my first encounter with black American teenagers, as well as my face-to face encounter with the real American underclass in Harlem, is vividly recounted in this chapter. An answer to the often asked question of whether Africans in the United States are treated any better than black Americans is also provided in this chapter. The chapter also presents some insight into the relationship between Africans and black Americans in the United States.

NOTE

1. Gatheru Mungo, an African, recounts similar feelings upon his arrival in the United States in his book, *Child of Two Worlds -- A Kikiyu's Story* (Garden City, N.J.: Anchor Books, 1965), p. 148.

Chapter 1

America the Beautiful

"God has smiled on our Undertaking"

In an appearance on a Donahue talk show in which he was discussing the role of the United States in world affairs, Bishop Desmond Tutu, the South African freedom fighter and 1984 Nobel Peace Laureate, referred to the United States as "God's own country." Casual as the statement might have been, the statement can be considered very important for at least two reasons. First, Bishop Tutu may very well have been reflecting the perceptions of many people in the rest of the world, especially the developing world. Thus, his statement clearly emphasizes the importance the world attaches to the United States. How else is the rest of the world, particularly the developing world, supposed to explain America's spectacular economic, technological, scientific, and material progress?

The second reason, and perhaps even more important, is that Bishop Tutu's description of America fits very well the image and perception of what many Americans really consider their country to be -- God's own country. Indeed, since the creation of this country, many Americans have thought of themselves as God's chosen people. Abraham Lincoln in 1863, for example, declared, "We have been the *recipients of the choicest bounties of heaven. We have been preserved, these many years, in peace and prosperity. We have grown in numbers, wealth and power, as no other nation has ever grown*"[1] (emphasis mine). But Americans not only believe that they have specially been chosen by God, but also that there is an international dimension to their concept of "manifest destiny," a doctrine that posits that America has a special responsibility to educate the world, christianize the heathen world, and to ensure the survival of democracy, the oil that greases the capitalist state machinery, throughout the world. For many Americans, theirs is a city-state set up on the mountain top to look over the world. In his book, *Our Country*, Josiah Strong argued that Americans possessed "an instinct or genius for colonization." He claimed that "God with infinite wisdom and skill is training the Anglo-Saxon race for the final competition of values" and that soon American civilization would "move down upon" Mexico and Latin America and "out upon the islands of the sea, over Africa and beyond."[2] A recent manifestation of this "manifest destiny" is the "international policeman" role that the United States has assumed without any challenge, especially in the post Cold War era. Recent examples of this policeman role include the invasion of Grenada, the arrest and detention of the president of Panama, General Noriega, the conquest of Iraq in the Gulf War, the dispatch of U.S. troops to Somalia and Haiti. As a self-styled international policeman, the United States has conferred on itself the power to intervene in other countries' internal affairs to dispense "American justice" as it deems fit and to spread America's concept of democracy and capitalism around the world. The United States has sought to do this with contempt and religious fervor. And the price for those who don't share these American perceptions has been rather great.

Although many Americans would argue that their doctrine of manifest destiny is distinct from the European imperialist activities around the world at the turn of the century, the reality is that the United States used military power to take the Hawaiian Islands, Guam, Puerto Rico, Cuba, and the Philippines. Whatever moralistic pronouncements America may make on its doctrine of manifest destiny did not stop it from invading practically every country in Latin America - Cuba, Colombia, Nicaragua, Haiti, Panama, Grenada, El Salvador, and others - all in the name of "protecting democracy."

In some cases, the use of "American justice" has gone to a dangerous precedent-setting extreme, such as was the case when the head of state of Panama, General Noriega, was arrested, tried by American law, convicted, and finally, jailed in an America prison. For Americans, expansionism was associated with evangelism; the United States had a sacred responsibility, they believed, having been singled out by the divinity for the salvation of the planet. This rhetoric underscored Woodrow Wilson's pledge to "make the world safe for democracy under American auspices."[3]

For many people in Latin America, Africa, and most parts of Asia, an important question that has been appropriately asked is, Why are we being oppressed in the name of justice, enslaved in the name of freedom, murdered in the name of life? Perhaps, a more general question is, Why are we always being judged by American standards? Why are we being forced to live by America's sense of morality? Does the United States really have any moral, or indeed, any authority at all, to police the world? And what makes America feel that it can impose its value system on the rest of the world?

Whether or not Americans have the authority to police the world, much less impose its value on the rest of the world, the fact still remains that many Americans feel that they are superior to the rest of the world and that they have established the most civilized, powerful, and industrialized society, the like of which has never existed before and will never exist anywhere oilstone the world. In the United States, you only have to turn on your television to hear all manner of persons, ranging from politicians to movie stars, sports figures, ministers of the gospel, and so on, all lavishly praising and describing America in superlatives - the only superpower in the world, the most powerful industrial democracy, the freest people in the world, the richest country in the world, and the like.

In fact, the American baseball championship series, played only in the United States, is billed the "World Series" to underscore the point that there is no other world than the United States of America. Thus, when it happens in America, then obviously it has happened everywhere in the world! Yes, Americans are not modest people by any stretch of the imagination, at least not when it comes to indulging in national narcissism.

One is therefore inclined to ask, What is so great about America? And what keeps America great? One American writer describes the nation's greatness in the following way, "There is no question about the fact that America is a blessed country. It harbors a wealth of natural resources - the oil, the ore, the timber, the water, the soil, and the climate - all have combined to nourish a great civilization. These have also combined to produce agricultural abundance unparalleled anywhere else."[4]

There is some validity in the description above. For example, while half of the world's people go to bed hungry every night, most people in the United States live in economic abundance. America's per capita income of $19,840 is surpassed by only five countries in the world. America is viewed by many, including foreigners, as having been blessed with a heritage of hard work, dedication, generosity, and uncompromising desire for freedom and individual liberty. Thus, America at the age of only a little over two hundred years has built a military and economic power unparalleled in history. But these may still not adequately explain America's greatness. After all, Africa and many countries in Latin America have equally been endowed with tremendous natural resources, but the mere availability of natural resources has not necessarily produced economic or social prosperity in these regions. It seems therefore that America's economic prosperity may in part be accounted for by the kind of people who settled the United States and the types of institutions they set up to transform those natural resources to meet their needs.

To understand fully what makes America a great country, one needs to understand what makes a person an American and what historical and natural forces have created such a being. Understanding who is an American may well be the first step to understanding what makes the nation great. This is so because there are many different kinds of Americans, and there doesn't seem to be any consensus among all Americans as to what is great about their country or what keeps it great.

For example, can we call any person who acquires an American citizenship an American? Is an African or a Mexican who comes to the United States, marries an American, and acquires U.S. citizenship so that he can get a good job any less American than the immigrants who arrived on the *Mayflower*? Are the descendants of black Americans who were captured as slaves against their wish, brought forcefully onto slave ships, enslaved for decades, and forced by circumstances to become American citizens as much American citizens as the descendants of the Puritan immigrants who came to the United States willingly in search of a better life and for economic, political, and religious freedoms? Shall we expect these different Americans to share the same dreams, the same cultural and social values, to have the same perspective about things, and to be equally patriotic about their country?

To Malcolm X, for example, being born in the United States did not necessarily make people Americans, especially if they were black Americans.

In 1964 he said:

I am one who doesn't believe in deluding myself. Being born here in America doesn't make you an American. Why, if birth made you American, you wouldn't need any legislation, you wouldn't need any amendments to the constitution, you wouldn't be faced with civil-rights filibustering in Washington D.C., right now. They don't have to pass a civil rights legislation to make a Pollack an American. I'm one of the 22 million black people who are the victims of Americanism. I don't see any American dream; I see an American nightmare.[5]

As this quote makes obvious, perhaps citizenship implies something deeper than a legalistic attribute of place of birth or nationalistic sense of belonging. Is a redefinition of "American" called for as new immigrants make their way into the United States?

It appears that this question may have as much a legal dimension as emotional, cultural, and ethnographic dimensions. I strongly believe that an individual's view of the United States, whether real or distorted, is greatly influenced by ethnographic variables such as national origins; by religion; by demographic variables such as age, gender, and place of residence; and by social variables such as social, economic, and educational status. Being an American may well be more of a feeling or a state of mind than anything legalistic or ethnocentric. Does the African in the above quote, for instance, feel more as an African or an American most of the time? Does he act his Africanness and Americanness at different places and under different circumstances?

Some have argued that the American melting pot has been so successful that by the time a person is proclaimed an American citizen he or she must have melted into the mainstream of American life and behave the American way. This person must not only dream the all-American dream, but must also strive to attain it. The idea that the United States is a great melting pot was popularized by Israel Zangwill (1865-1926), the poet, novelist, and political activist, in one of his melodramas that opened in Washington, D.C., in 1908: "America is God's crucible, the great melting pot, where all the races of Europe are melting and reforming Germans and Frenchmen, Irishmen and Englishmen, Jews and Russians -- into the crucible with you all! God is making the American."[6]

Foreigners who accept U.S. citizenship are made to take a test in which they are supposed to learn about American history, politics, and culture and value systems. Those who cannot pass the test are theoretically unqualified to be American. The assumption is that the "newest" American citizen must embody the same basic values as the Founding Fathers so as to permit continuity and progress. After all, if the values of the Founding Fathers are responsible for America's greatness, then for the United States to continue to go forward, all those who would choose to call themselves Americans must of necessity imbibe these values!

Historians have done a good job in analyzing the factors or forces that have produced and shaped the modern American. Some of these historians have argued that something in the American environment had transformed the otherwise weary and broken Europeans who made it to the United States into energetic, proud and successful builders of a modern Western civilization. Others, however, have argued that perhaps the men who came to America from Europe were different from those who stayed behind, and that in general, the strong, the brave, the daring, the innovative, and the wise were the ones who dared to come to the wild virgin country.

Many have also argued that perhaps what makes the United States a great nation lies in the institutions and the value systems that the country upholds. Those who subscribe to this view would strongly argue that America's greatest strength may not lie in its military and economic might, nor in its industrial and technological prowess, but in its institutions and value systems -- democracy, liberty, individualism, free enterprise, sense of fairness, justice, hard work, innovativeness, equality of opportunity, generosity, and a competitive spirit. But how did these institutions and value systems develop, and are these tenable in modern America?

I find it unnecessary to engage in a detailed discussion of the historical and political development of American institutions and value systems since it is only tangential to the purpose of this chapter. However, it is important to state that the United States had its beginning in resistance against religious oppression and a revolt against suppression of personal liberty.

This resentment of attempts to suppress religious dissent was buttressed by a nationalistic desire for independence. A group of religious dissenters, for example, fled England in 1608 to escape religious persecution and settled near the mouth of the Hudson River. The values these Pilgrims brought with them became entrenched and formed the basis of American social, political, and economic cultures. For example, the *Mayflower* immigrants, it is argued, embodied a greater desire for freedom than perhaps any of the other immigrant groups.[7]

Before going ashore after docking accidentally on Cape Cod Bay, the Pilgrims drew up the Mayflower Compact. The Compact stated:

We whose names are underwritten do by these presents, solemnly and mutually in the presence of God and one another covenant and combine ourselves under into a civil Body Politick and by Virtue hereby do enact such just and equal laws . . . as shall be thought most meet and convenient for the general good of the colony.[8]

By committing themselves to the contents of this compact, "ordinary folks had created a government based on mutual respect and interdependence -- the beginnings of the development of American republican government and democracy."[9]

For the Puritans who had come to America to establish a purer society, God's blessings were expressed both materially and spiritually, and thus success in the accumulation of "worldly goods was likely although not necessary indication for salvation."[10] Accordingly, hard work, thrift, and strict adherence to business were qualities to be cultivated by those who hoped to enter heaven. The Puritans were therefore "preeminently behaviorist; they wanted to create a visible kingdom of God on earth," and that kingdom supposedly is "manifested" in the America we see today.[11]

It is also a truism that a nation is a sum of many influences, and certainly nothing is more important than the natural phenomenon of the country. Great as America's natural resources may well be, as Lyman Abbot stated, "A nation is made great not by its fruitful acres, but by the men who cultivate them, not by its great forests, but by the men who use them, not by its mines, but by the men who built and run them. America was a great land when Columbus discovered it: Americans have made it a great nation."[12]

America is one of the most heterogenous countries in the world. The immigrants who came to America had many different origins, religions, and life-styles, yet they were bound together by a common purpose, wish, and aspiration. They were motivated by freedom, liberty, individualism, personal achievement, an incredible urge to explore a new frontier, and the ever present challenge of the unknown. As Frederick Jackson Turner wrote, "The spirit that fired the American mind was the fact of an expanding frontier." They were the tired, the poor, and the huddled masses, yet they brought valuable skills, hope, energy, fresh perspective, and, above all, new determination. The immigrants worked long hours. They had a virgin, barren country, with tremendous natural resources, a country that needed building, and they went about it seriously. The fruit of their effort has been manifested in the transformation of a rough, virgin, and sometimes dangerous country into a "superpower," a nation, most Americans believe, that is the most industrialized country in the world.

Thus, America has successfully modeled a society of people from all over the world. It is also sometimes argued that strangers are not supposed to set up civilizations together. Some would even say that a nation must arise out of a tribe, or perhaps, out of a greater affinity, such as blood, but the United States with its great polyglot of ingathering has done well without either. The melting pot appears to have melted brilliantly to produce a desirable outcome.

As can be deduced from the above, the early American immigrants believed that democracy, religious freedom, liberty, and material success were ideals worth preserving, and if they could be won only through wars so be it! Thus, America may have come to its people not as a gift of fortune, but as a result of dedication to duty and hard work and a conquering spirit that appeared to have characterized the early American ethos and the American culture in general. Armed with these ideals, value system, and deism -- a faith that revered God for the marvels of His universe rather than for His power over humankind -- Americans were determined to conquer nature, mankind, or anything that stood in their way to material and technological progress. Institutionalization and aggressive cultivation of the values of democracy, capitalism, freedom, liberty, individualism, and the establishment of a republican government were deemed necessary to ensure the survival and protection of these values.

In the pursuit of these ideals and goals, war with others was inevitable. It can be said that war has profoundly affected the American character. Americans have supposedly fought for religious freedom and for the protection of democracy around the world. The United States has paid the price with American lives -- one hundred twenty thousand in World War I, forty thousand in World War II, fifty-four thousand in Korea, and fifty-six thousand in Vietnam -- supposedly in the name of freedom. However, it is not the number of casualties that is remarkable, but the apparent zeal and dedication -- the belief in and the commitment to the ideal of freedom and its preservation. To many Americans, no price is too great for freedom.

One of the most moving periods of my stay in this country occurred during an interview of an American mother who had just lost her son in the bombing of the United States marine headquarters in Beirut in 1984. Responding to an interviewer's question about how she felt about the death of her son, the mother responded without any regret or anger, "I am proud that my son died to preserve freedom. Whoever said that freedom was free?" This may well have summarized the feeling of many Americans as to their perceived role in maintaining freedom around the world at whatever cost.

Individualism and free enterprise march at the same beat. And many Americans I have met attribute their country's greatness to its emphasis on individualism, liberty, justice, and a free enterprise economic system. In a recent survey that I conducted among my students, faculty, church members, and some street people, a majority of the respondents ranked these values as the greatest virtue of the American society. I then posed the question, "What is freedom, individualism, and the free enterprise economic system?"

To many of these Americans, individualism implies the ability to pursue one's interest without hindrance; to develop one's potential to the greatest possible limit without conformity; and, to be able to maintain one's individuality and identity. It is argued that individualism, or the struggle to attain it, is what propels innovativeness and inventiveness. It thus turns the wheels of the free enterprise economic system.

Free enterprise -- capitalism, as it is most often referred to - is pursued with the same fervor in the United States as religion. Everything is denominated in dollars and cents -- politics, education, social status, love, and even family relationships. The profit motive underlies all economic and social relationships in this country and invariably provides all the various freedoms that America has come to be associated with, namely economic, political, and social freedoms.

For many Americans, money can buy any and everything, including love. The belief that runs through all social and economic programs in the United States is that if you throw enough money at a problem you can eventually solve it. As the discussions above show, the strength and greatness of the United States revolve around political and social freedoms and free enterprise.

America's ability to maintain its greatness is due in great part to its ability to relentlessly and endlessly reinvent itself and to keep in motion. With a devout belief in the inevitability of progress and a strong sense of self-criticism, the nation possesses an incredible resiliency of spirit and a fantastic ability to emerge stronger out of practically every disaster. Two recent examples illustrate this ability. The first deals with the effect of the Vietnam War on American society and the image consequently created about the United States around the world.

After much soul searching, self-recrimination, and heated public debates that nearly tore the country apart and destroyed its democratic institutions, America not only finally accepted the defeat, but also acknowledged that it had made mistakes in Vietnam and took appropriate measures to ensure that such mistakes would be avoided in the future.

Its public acknowledgment of its mistakes in Vietnam and its determination to avoid a repetition of such mistakes are clearly strengths that can come only from its democratic culture. This is captured most vividly by what Henry Kissinger, former U.S. secretary of state, said of the Vietnam War.

Vietnam is still with us. It has created doubts about American judgement, about American credibility, about American power -- not only at home, but throughout the world. It has poisoned our domestic debate. So we paid an exorbitant price for the decisions that were made in good faith and for good purpose.[13]

It is only after such clear public admission that mistakes have been made that the healing process can begin, and effective measures can be taken to avoid similar mistakes in the future.

With this admission, America was ready to put the war behind it and to move forward. Its ability to look forward, to make something positive out of a bad situation, was echoed by President Jerry Ford when he stated, "Today, America can regain the sense of pride that existed before Vietnam. But it cannot be achieved by refighting a war that is finished. These events, tragic as they are, portend neither the end of the world nor of America's leadership in the world."[14]

The second example is the U.S. ability to reinvent itself and to move forward in the aftermath of the Challenger space accident. Believing that there is no problem without a solution, when the Challenger accident occurred in 1986, President Ronald Reagan and the American people committed themselves to an overhauling of an otherwise safe and successful space program to avoid similar future accidents. In other cultures, this isolated accident may have been viewed as an aberration - something that would never happen again. That would not have been the American way. The whole space program was put on hold until new research was completed and a new type of "O" ring was developed before another space flight was permitted. I have always wondered what Americans would have done if their country had been subjected to the numerous military interventions that have clearly proven to be detrimental to the economic, social, and political development of Africa.

Would Americans have totally reorganized the institutional structure of the armed forces? Would they have changed the way their armed forces are trained and the command structure of the military? Would they have provided more public education about the role of the military in nation building? Would they have changed the tenure of service in the military and required military service for all its citizens? I believe they would have. These problems continue to afflict Africa, yet no serious attempts are being made to devise effective solutions. Within the African armed forces, it is considered taboo even to talk about coups, even though they pose the greatest threat to the armed forces itself as an institution and continue to be a clear and present danger to every country on the African continent.

Whatever basis is used to explain who an American is, and how he is different from his European ancestors, the Americans whom I have known, first as an exchange student in an American high school, then as a college student, and now as a college professor, are as ordinary as any other human beings. They are neither saviors of humankind nor any more godly or God's own than an African or any other human being. Americans, like all human beings, do have a sense of pain and feeling, can offer comfort and inflict pain, can be humane, and yet very cruel, can be gentle, and yet very violent.

If Americans are as common as any other human beings and are not inherently superior to any other people, as I believe is the case, then what explains America's spectacular successes in science and technology, in agriculture and commerce, and the tremendous material and economic success enjoyed by its people? And why has the United States accomplished so much more than most countries?

A critical examination of the value systems that are generally associated with Americans -- democracy, individualism, justice, liberty, hard work, thrift, enterprise, and so on -- would show that these values are similarly shared by other countries and cultures, including Africa and other developing countries. For example, I know from my personal experience and observation in the United States that many Africans are just as hard working as most Americans.

Unfortunately, Africa's unwillingness or slowness in adopting the Western way of life, the civil wars that continue to plague the continent in the aftermath of colonialism, Western television images of starving women and children, and the difficult economic circumstances that have militated against all attempts at economic development on the continent have all contributed to a cruel perception in the West that Africans are lazy and stupid. But this is not true.

The peasant farmers whom I left behind in Ghana are neither lazy nor stupid. They walk several miles on foot each morning to their farms, and with their primitive hoes and cutlasses, they work from morning till evening without the benefit of a clock to tell the time. They quit only when it is too dark to see anymore. These peasant farmers, again using their primitive cutlasses and hoes, for example, made Ghana the leading world producer of cocoa for so many years. The history of African slaves in the United States and elsewhere clearly demonstrates that African slaves were physically stronger and much more hard working than most of their white counterparts. This is one reason why they were most sought after. The problem for the African workers or the peasant farmers is that they are just not as productive as their western counterparts who have benefited greatly from their vast technological advances, which have effectively supplemented the efforts of Western workers, thus making them more productive.

Similarly, Africa's precolonial history shows that African village communities were fiercely democratic, with rights and obligations clearly specified and enforced. The Ibos of Nigeria, for example, had elaborate self-rule democratic institutions that allowed each member of the village to attend a village assembly and to participate in discussion of issues that affected the general well-being of the community. The description of the work of the Ibo assembly that follows, illustrates the type of grass roots democracy that was most common in many African village communities before the advent of colonialism. In the Ibo assembly, every man had the right to speak, the people applauding popular proposals and shouting down unpopular ones. Decisions had to be unanimous, and it was here that the young or wealthy men with records of service or dedication to the village could influence policy. If the elders tried to enforce an unpopular decision the young men could prevent any decision through the operation of the unanimous rule. If the ama-ala, the council of Elders, acted arbitrarily and refused to call the assembly, the people could demand it by completely ignoring them and bringing town life to a halt. The village assembly was considered the Ibo man's birthright, the guarantee of his rights, his shield against oppression, and the expression of his individualism.[15]

A review of other American values vis-á-vis African values would also show that most American values are not necessarily unique to Americans alone. Perhaps the reason why these values have had much greater impact on America's economic and social life is that not only have these values become institutionalized, but also there is a tremendous commitment to ensure that they are respected, enforced, and defended from abuse in the United States. In contrast, they have neither been effectively institutionalized or defended from abuse in Africa. For example, Africa's inability to institutionalize democratic values, such as freedom of speech, expression, and opinion, and to establish an independent judiciary system to dispense justice to protect life, liberty, freedom, and property has culminated instead in the establishment of military and civilian authoritarian, autocratic, and oligarchic rule throughout the African continent.

Restrictions on individual freedom and lack of protection for private property in particular have had tremendous negative effects on Africa's ability to be innovative and to develop the spirit of adventure. The lack of a democratic culture allows African leaders to declare themselves life-presidents and enables them to kill their own citizens, to steal the wealth of their citizens, and otherwise impoverish their people. This same lack of a democratic culture has closed all avenues for peaceful political change in Africa. As a result, civil wars and strife are the only viable means to effect a change of government, making coup d'etat the order of the day.

The critical issue in Africa today is good governance. This concerns the need for government to provide the appropriate institutional structures that ensure full and effective participation of the governed in the decision-making process, and to ensure respect for and guarantee fundamental human rights and freedoms of the individual. But how can one expect good governance from a government that can't be criticized and has no sense of responsibility to the governed as is the case in most African countries?

Again, as noted earlier, the early American immigrants were motivated by a love for freedom and independence; they were people who fled from religious oppression to obtain more freedom and liberty in the United States. Although no one can dispute the fact that Americans are known to love their freedom, and independence, and to cherish their individualism, many Americans also tend to believe that these are uniquely American traits that are seldom exhibited by peoples from the rest of the world, especially by Africans. For example, David Lamb, an American writer in his book, *The African*, talks about "the silent obedience so many Africans will pay their rulers, no matter how despotic or unrealistic their ways."[16] This is a misconception.

Africans in their precolonial days, as manifested in the above Ibo experience, shared similar democratic values with the West. Africans, like the Americans, were also ever prepared to stand up for their rights, dignity, and beliefs. Africa's precolonial history clearly shows that the Africans, for example, never thought of themselves as being in any way inferior to the Europeans. On the contrary, they thought that given the opportunity to develop their own indigenous economic, social, and political institutions they could be just as progressive as the Europeans.

Africans were therefore not only optimistic of the future, but were also defiant of white intrusion and ready to defend their sovereignty and way of life. The African mood at the time just before colonialism is best captured by an exchange that took place between Mchemba, king of Yao, in modern Tanzania, and the German commander, Hermann Von Wissmann, in 1890:

I have listened to your words but can find no reason why I should obey you -- I would rather die first. If it should be friendship that you desire, then I am ready for it, today and always; but to be your subject, that I cannot be. If it should be war that you desire, then I am ready, but never to be your subject. I do not fall at your feet, for you are God's creature just as I am. I am Sultan here in my land. You are Sultan there in yours. Yet, I do not say to you that you should obey me; for I know that you are a free man.[17]

Similarly, in 1891, when the British offered protection to the Asantehene, Prempeh 1, he refused it in order to maintain the independence and sovereignty of his kingdom. His reply to the British was as follows:

The suggestion that Asante in its present state should come and enjoy the protection of her Majesty the Queen and Empress of India is a matter of very serious consideration. My Kingdom of Asante will never commit itself to any such policy. Asante must remain as of old, at the same time to remain friendly with all white men.[18]

At the risk of oversimplifying the point of the discussion above, the difference between Africans and Americans is not that Americans are any more hard working than Africans, nor that Americans love freedom, liberty, justice, fairness, or individualism more than the Africans do. The difference is that Americans realized much more quickly the weakness of man and the potential corrupting nature of power. Thus, they took the appropriate measures to limit the powers of government and made sure that the appropriate institutions were built and strengthened to protect the values they cherished most.

It needs to be strongly emphasized that I do not for a minute believe that democracy by itself would have ensured economic and material prosperity for Africa. Democracy offers opportunities only for free people, working together, to govern themselves in ways that most facilitate the achievement of their own goals and promote justice, personal freedoms, and economic opportunities. If these values are cherished and protected, then the enabling environment is created that can lead to economic development and material success. To the extent that these values have been proscribed, as has been the case in Africa, personal dictatorships and political instability have filled the vacuum.

Americans, for example, enacted laws that protected them against political abuse, guaranteed freedom and liberty, and individualism. Africans also shared and equally cherished these values but lost them during the colonial period and never recovered them after colonialism. In other words, the ability of Americans to breathe life into the values they espoused has contributed significantly to their success story. This is where Africa failed most.

As the earlier quotations from the two great African kings show, some Africans resisted colonialism and its encroachment on their freedoms, dignity, culture, and value systems. Even after having been conquered and colonized, Africans were quite optimistic that their freedoms would be restored when they regained their independence. In Ghana the rallying battle cry during the struggle for independence was "Freedom and justice." Africans, it was argued then, must be free to govern themselves, to make and pay for their own mistakes, to learn and to grow from their own experience. But above all, Africans needed to be free from the injustices, humiliation, abuses, and subjugation of colonialism. Upon attainment of independence, justice would flow from the mighty Atlantic ocean, and with that progress, peace, and prosperity would come. These noble virtues and expectations of most Africans I am sure were equally shared by the Founding Fathers of the United States.

But today there is neither freedom nor justice on the vast African continent. Africans have neither freedoms nor justice because the freedoms gained from the white colonialists at the time of independence were quickly seized by black indigenous "colonialists." Leaders who could earn neither the respect nor the admiration of their peoples forced themselves on Africa.

At the time when the American Founding Fathers were looking for ways to curtail the encroachment of governmental powers on individual rights, and when Thomas Jefferson was issuing a disclaimer on the virtues of big government and declaring any government a necessary evil at best due to its nature to restrict the freedom of the individual, African governments were actively dismantling multiparty democratic systems inherited from the colonial period, consolidating authoritarianism, and planting the roots of presidential cultism.

As it happened, then, in the early days of the nation-building process, while Americans were channeling their energies into building institutions that would eventually facilitate their development, Africans, ironically, were destroying their institutions and channeling their energies into tribalism, civil wars, and civil strife. In my judgment, therefore, there is nothing inherently superior about the American as a human being as much as it is about American institutions.

The differences in the institutions of government between Africa and the United States account for the significant difference between Africa's dismal economic and technological performance, and America's spectacular performance in the field of economics, science, and technology. As an African, an outsider, looking into the American society, I see America's greatest strength in its democratic institutions; if there was one thing that I could carry back with me to Africa that certainly is what I would choose. American technology is in part derived from the nation's sense of the inevitability of progress, a feeling that every problem has a solution. This comes from the ability to perform without hindrance and unnecessary rules and regulations.

American democracy and other value systems may have their own failings, as we will see momentarily when we examine the extent to which American values are shared and applied to non-Caucasian Americans and people from the rest of the world. In spite of any obvious failings, the United States' institutionalization of its democratic values and subsequent development of a democratic culture have enabled it to be its own best critic, which in turn has enabled it to constantly reinvent itself. It is in these terms that Carlos Fuentes sees America's greatness, greatness that comes from its "democratic process, its capacity for self government, self negation, even self flagellation, and self consciousness.[19] On this matter, there is very little disagreement. However, regarding the universality of the application and sharing of America's values, there is much to disagree with.

Earlier, in my discussion of American ideals, values and institutions, I raised the issue regarding the degree of the United States' commitment to its value systems and ideals when it came to dealing with non-Caucasian Americans and other races, especially those from the developing world. I personally have always felt that many of the American values and ideals that have been cited above as the cornerstone of America's greatness can be challenged in terms of their practical application, as well as in terms of America's depth of commitment to them, both within and outside its borders. For example, can America claim to provide equal opportunity to all of its citizens?

Can America claim any serious depth of commitment to justice and fairness when women and minorities, for example, performing the same work with male Caucasians are in some cases paid 30 percent less? Can there be justice and fairness when people are discriminated against on the basis of their sex, or the color of their skin? For the outsider looking into the American pluralistic society, the American conception of freedom and democracy can be quite troubling too.

The contradictions seem overwhelming. For example, recall the mother who is satisfied that her son died fighting for freedom in Beirut. For the outsider, perhaps even for any non-Caucasian American, the simple question is, What kind of freedom was the son fighting for, and for whom was the freedom being fought? Again, it may be asked, What kind of democracy was America trying to restore in Viet Nam that was worth forty-six thousand American lives, over three hundred thousand casualties, a cost of over $109 billion at the end of the war in 1973 and millions in Vietnamese lives? What kind of democracy was America defending in Iran when it protected Shah Palavi? When it protected President Marcos and his cronies in the Philippines? When it protected the bloodthirsty Pinochet in Chile? When it supported the Papa Doc and Baby Doc Duvalier dynasty in Haiti? For many, the United States was not fighting for the principles and ideals that it stands for on their own merit as much as it was fighting to protect its economic and strategic interests in all of these countries. A common statement heard in the United States during the Vietnam War in the 1960s, and the Persian Gulf war in 1991 was, "Poor blacks fighting against browns in the interest of rich whites."

For many outside observers, U.S. military intervention in foreign countries has little to do with seeking to establish or protect American values or ideals for the indigenous people in the countries it intervenes. Fuentes appeared to speak for many in the developing world when he said that the United States is "a democracy inside, but an empire outside."[20]   This sentiment, shared by many from the developing world may well explain the love -- hate feelings that many of these people have for the United States.

Again, Fuentes aptly stated this feeling when he said, "While I admire America's democratic achievements and the cultural values of its society, we will continue to oppose its arrogant and violent policies in Latin America. We will do so *painfully, because we love so many things in the United States*"[21] (emphasis mine). I, like Fuentes, love so many things about the United States but resent the double standards that it applies in its dealings with the rest of the world, especially the developing world.

America is indeed full of contradictions, and it is these contradictions that allow it to be generous on one hand and greedy on the other; to defend the right of an unborn fetus on one hand and yet to murder and abuse millions of innocent children every year; to capture and enslave Africans and yet fight for democracy, justice, and liberty for the Europeans. For many outsiders, the United States acts like "Dr. Jekyll at home and Mr. Hyde outside."

America also prides itself as a fair and just society, but even within its own borders, these concepts of fairness and justice that are supposed to ensure the attainment of the American dream are limited in their scope of application. It is assumed in America that with Americans being generally fair and the legal system being just, a person needs only to work hard and he or she will attain the American dream. But is this really true? This is true depending on your socioeconomic-ethnic class, and your social standing in the community, if not solely on the color of your skin.

Martin Luther King, Jr., for example, challenged America's lack of a universal adherence to justice and fairness when he stated, "Injustice anywhere is a threat to justice everywhere." Here, King was implying that the United States cannot go to war to defend justice in one place and blatantly ignore it in another place. So it has been asked over and over again, "Can people be asked to fight for justice for others when they are deprived of the same?" In other words, can black Americans be asked to fight for democracy and justice for Nicaraguans, for Vietnamese, for Grenadines, for Kuwaitis, and for Koreans, when they are themselves denied justice on the basis of their skin color? Is justice gained in Korea or Kuwait at the expense of justice in the United States worth fighting for at all, or even worth preserving?

Again, individualism is another value that many Americans describe as being important for their nation's accomplishments and something that makes the United States different from other countries. Almost all my students have been unanimous in their praise of the United States for providing the greatest opportunity for individuals to retain their individuality -- the opportunity to be what they want to be, without any institutionalized processes or mechanisms to force anyone to conform to any set standard but their own, within the limits of the law. Again, the reality is different from the ideal. And the reality is that all the immigrants to the United States have been forced to adapt to the dominant Euro-American culture and value system or "perish."

Black Americans, for example, whose cultural identity is far different from the Euro-American culture, have been forced to become bicultural. C. Valentine makes the case that the "collective behavior and social life of the black American community is bicultural in the sense that each black American ethnic segment draws upon both a distinctive repertoire of standardized black American behaviors and, simultaneously, patterns drawn from the dominant culture."[22]

R. Staples argues that the "bicultural nature of black Americans is something forced upon them and is often antithetical to their own values." He further claims that black American commitment to Euro-American values is not necessarily positive, and although African Americans may engage in Euro-American cultural practices, such as materialism, this should not be taken as a strong commitment to those values.[23] For the black American, therefore, there appears to be a conflict between choosing to behave in the "black way" and the "nonblack way" depending on the circumstances.[24]

Similarly, a great deal is made of equality in the United States. The very word invites polemic. Nearly fifty years ago Gunnar Myrdal made the observation, really an indictment, that "The economic situation for the negroes in America is pathological."[25] Of course, some improvements have been made, but for the majority of the over 25 million black Americans in the United States, the change has not been significant. Yes, since then America has done well to dismantle many of the legal racial barriers that limited social, economic, and residential mobility. And black success can be seen in the increased number of state and federal congressional delegates.

President Clinton's cabinet includes four African Americans, with important portfolios such as commerce and agriculture. The former chairman of America's Joint Chiefs of Staff, General Colin Powell, is also black. In the field of sports and entertainment, blacks have excelled, with Michael Jordan and Janet Jackson being among the highest paid people in the world. At the same time, over the past two decades, the size of the black middle class has expanded and grown much faster than the white middle class, with the proportion of blacks earning more than $50,000 a year (in 1990 dollars) increasing by 46 percent compared with only a 35 percent increase among white families.[26]

This progress notwithstanding, there is still a growing inequality in the black community. For example, as successful blacks got richer, the unsuccessful ones got even more marginalized. A visit to the slums of South Chicago and New York, only a few miles from the soaring skyscrapers and spectacular shops in downtown Chicago and Manhattan, respectfully, will dramatize the weight of this inequality. With its crime, drugs, prostitution, violence, and insect-infested apartments, life in these ghettos cuts blacks off not only from the rest of America, but mentally and emotionally. What many white Americans regard as pathological -- "unemployment, unwed childbearing, welfare dependency, drug-taking, violent crime -- is regarded as routine of the ghetto life."[27]

In 1992 the U.S. census data showed that 46 percent of black American family households were headed by single women. Children from these single-parent and impoverished homes are at least twice as likely to suffer from serious health problems as their white counterparts, and the mother is more than twice as likely to be addicted to alcohol or drugs.[28]

This alienation and isolation is not exclusive only to the black underclass. It is pervasive even within the black middle class. A recent study by Douglas Massey on geographical segregation in the United States concluded, "middle class blacks are only marginally less segregated than poor blacks." Middle-class blacks live overwhelmingly in black suburbs. It appears today that whites are happy to live with blacks only if the blacks are less than 8 percent of the population in that given area. The suburban housing markets work to ensure that this maximum is not exceeded. Whenever the proportion of blacks exceeds 8 percent, then whites start moving out, property prices tumble, and the neighborhood becomes all-black.[29]

This residential segregation, or prejudice appears to be uniquely directed against blacks. Whites do not complain much and even seem happy to allow other minorities (other than blacks) to move in with them. In Los Angeles, the poorest Latinos are now barely more segregated than the richest blacks.[30]

The question that continues to be raised about black Americans is, can they achieve and live the American dream, the accomplishment of which itself requires them to become fully integrated into the white society, and to embrace and imbibe the Euro-American culture and value system? In other words, can black Americans achieve the American dream and yet keep their identity intact? Can they achieve economic and material success in the face of racism that has caused them to consistently "experience higher rates of joblessness, underemployment, high mortality, morbidity, family instability and broken homes, poor housing, homicide, and institutionalization rates much higher than their white counterparts?"[31] Obviously, the answer is no.

As a solution, conformity rather than individuality is increasingly being preached to black Americans and other recent immigrants to the United States. For black Americans, Myrdal offered, "It is to the advantage of the American Negroes as individuals and as a group to be assimilated into the American culture, to acquire the traits held in *esteem* by the dominant culture."[32] (emphasis mine)

This dilemma is also faced by other recent immigrants to the United States. For recent African and Latin American immigrants who have arrived in the United States with strong cultural and value systems held intact and would like to maintain them, it has been an agonizing decision -- to abandon either the culture of the "old country" in favor of economic prosperity in the "new country" or to continue to hold onto the cultural and value systems of the old country and pay the ultimate economic price -- foregoing any prospects of ever achieving the "American dream." This agonizing choice which invariably faces all non-European immigrants to the United States, is well treated by Gatheru Murgo in his book, *Child of Two Worlds*. In the book, Murgo, who was an African student in the United States during the 1960s, talked a great deal about the dilemma of being torn between African values and the Euro-American values. He referred to himself and others like him as "the child of two worlds," needing to learn the American way of doing things in order to advance socially and economically.

For the outsider, especially people from the developing world who are subjected to economic deprivation, denied political and social freedoms, and besieged by civil wars and civil strife, America will continue to be the land of promise and of opportunity, a place where dreams can come true; the land where people with humble beginnings and backgrounds, such as mine, can come, work hard, and achieve the American dream. Indeed, millions in the developing world, as well as in the developed world, are struggling to come to the United States. *Newsweek* recently reported that six Chinese would-be immigrants to the United States died in their desperate attempt to swim 200 yards to what they viewed as "Meiguo," the beautiful country (the United States), after their shipwreck.[33]   These immigrants paid between $20,000 to $50,000 to be smuggled into the United States.[34]

The acting chair of the United States Commission on Immigration reform, Lawrence Fauchs, estimates that five hundred thousand illegal aliens enter the United States each year. According to Fauche, "the glitter of materialism on American television shows is responsible" to a large extent for the wave of migration to the United States.[35] The question that will continue to haunt all would-be immigrants to the United States is whether they will achieve the American dream, or instead see an American nightmare.

Increasingly, the American dream is getting beyond the reach of many immigrants to the United States. Even when the dream is achieved, it appears that the price paid for its achievement is too high.   For many of these immigrants, the reality in today's America can be illustrated with a joke told to me by an Indian friend. In comparing the differences between the image and perception held by outsiders about America and the reality that exists in America today, he told this joke. A man who had been very good while alive passed away.   After being escorted by a guide to Heaven, he came across two waystations. The first one had a signboard signifying Heaven. He peeked through a small hole and saw many people sitting around.

Some were reading books, and others appeared to be working hard at various jobs. He walked up to the next waystation, on which there was a signboard with a bold inscription, Hell. He similarly peeked through a small hole, but this time found many people dancing and generally having a good time. He was impressed and promptly decided that he preferred to go to Hell.

His guide could not believe him. He cautioned, "You have lived a good life and you deserve to go to Heaven, please, do not go to Hell." But he would not be convinced. The poor man was thus sent to Hell. When he got there, he found nothing but suffering -- people screaming in pain, people being tortured and being shot to death. He could not believe what he was seeing. He went to the officer in charge and said to him, "Sir, I think something is wrong here. This is not what I saw through the small hole or heard about this place. I am a good man and deserve something better than this." The officer looked at the poor man and said, "What you saw through the small hole was our public relations office's advertisement. What you are seeing here is the reality. And remember, reality is always different from what you see or hear."

This joke in many ways dramatizes the perceptions of many immigrants of the American society and the realities of life in the United States. In many cases, perception is quite different from reality.   And reality in the United States, like that in many countries, in many cases, depends on who you are and where you are at a particular point in time.

Thus it has been for the millions of immigrants for whom the American dream has become a nightmare. And similarly, for many Americans who have attained the dream, the price of success, as we will read in the next chapter, may have been too high. If economic and material success was supposed to free Americans from the present, it certainly has succeeded in enslaving Americans to the future.

NOTES

1. *The Rebirth of America* (Philadelphia: Arthur DeMoss Foundation, 1986), p. 151.

2. John A. Garraty, *Our Country* (1855), *The American Nation* (New York: Harper & Row, 1983), p. 542.

3. Stanley Karnow, *Vietnam: A History* (New York: Viking Press, 1983), p. 13.

4. *The Rebirth of America*, p. 23.

5. From *Malcom X Speaks* (New York: Grove Press, 1965). Quoted in Mark West, ed., *The Asheville Reader: The Future and the Individual* (Acton, Mass.: Copley Publishing Group, 1992) p. 74.

6. *Newsweek*, August 9, 1993, p. 16.

7. John A. Garraty, *The American Nation* (New York: Harper & Row, 1983), p. 16.

8. Ibid., p. 17.

9. Ibid.

10. Ibid., p. 43.

11. Ibid.

12. *The Rebirth of America*, p. 23.

13. Karnow, *Vietnam*, p. 9.

14. Ibid., p. 623.

15. Basil Davidson, *The Africans* (London: Longmans, Green & Co., Ltd., 1969), p. 93.

16. David Lamb, *The Africans* (New York: Random House, 1982), p. 51.

17. Davidson, p. 23.

18. Ibid., p. 24.

19. Carlos Fuentes, "The Land of Jekyll and Hyde," *The Nation* 242 (March 22, 1986). Reprinted in *The Asheville Reader* (Acton, Mass.: Copley Publishing, 1992), p. 39.

20. Ibid., p. 40.

21. Ibid.

22. Quoted in Don Locke, *Increasing Multicultural Understanding* (Newbury Park, Calif.: Sage Publications, 1992) p. 16

23. Ibid., p. 16

24. Ibid., p. 16

25. Quoted in *Economist*, July 10, 1993, p. 17

26. Ibid., p. 17

27. Ibid., p. 17

LIBRARY

28. Ibid., p. 17

29. Ibid., p. 17

30. Ibid., p. 17

31. Locke, p. 17

32. Gunnar Myrdal, *An American Dilemma* (New York: Harper & Row, 1944), p. 929

33. *Newsweek*, June 21, 1993 p. 36

34. Ibid., p. 36

35. *Newsweek*, August 9, 1993, p. 20

Chapter 2

What Price Success?

America's impressive military victory over Iraq in the Persian Gulf War appears to many, including Americans themselves, as testimony of America's military and technological superiority. Many Americans saw this victory as necessary to restore America's confidence; to exorcise the self-doubt that had lingered since the post Vietnam defeat. For many others, this victory was necessary to reassure the United States of its preeminence in a world increasingly dominated by Japan's economic and technological power.

For many people, however, especially those from the developing world--those outside looking in--there has never been any doubt about America's place in the world. For many of these people, the view is that the God of American destiny has answered all of America's prayers, perhaps beyond the wildest imagination of the Americans themselves.

Many see America as having been given "domination" over all the things that move on the face of the earth. Few realize, however, that no success is without its price. America's great achievements in science and technology, agriculture and industry, economic and material well-being, military and political influence have all been attained at the greatest price in terms of crime and violence, fractured family lives, drug addiction and alcoholism, apathy and greed, health problems, environmental damage and many untold human, social, and economic problems. In this chapter I examine how America's economic, material, political and technological successes have impacted on the American society and way of life.

It is a great irony that the very things that make the United States such a great nation are the very things that cause its great failings as an industrialized, civilized, and technologically superior nation. It is equally ironic that the problems in this country generally result not from want of food, shelter, and other basic necessities of life but from America's economic and material abundance, overemphasis on personal freedoms and liberty, individualism, optimism, hard work, competitive spirit, emphasis on personal success, and achievement and technological progress. Daniel Boorstin put it more simply, "I have long suspected that our problems arise less from our weaknesses than from our strengths. From our literacy, and wealth and optimism and progress."[1]

From its fragile beginnings, the great American promise was to open doors so that men and women could develop their individual potentials and follow their dreams and aspirations. To accomplish this promise, individual freedoms and liberty were necessary. Freedom, the most cherished ideal of America, allows the free movement of people, free speech, assembly, thought, religion, opportunity, justice, and the pursuit of life, liberty, and happiness among many others. America, a nation made up of perhaps one of the most heterogeneous peoples in the world including (ethnicity, beliefs, culture, and religion), could not have become a single nation if it had not recognized these rights and the right of every American to be equal, although they may be different from each other in race, religion, sex, and wealth.

Freedom offers possibilities, and Americans may be said to live on possibilities--virtually everything is possible in this country. It is possible for an aristocrat to become the president of this country, and so too it is possible for a peanut farmer to rise to the presidency of this Republic. It is even possible for a Hollywood movie star to become president of the same Republic. And it is only in America that a drifter can shoot the president, plead insanity, and be practically released.

Again, it is only in America that an entertainer can make $10 million in a single season and that a sports star can make even more millions in a single season, playing baseball, basketball, or football. It is this freedom of choice, of access to opportunities, of movement, and of expression, and more, that opens up all these possibilities.

I was born in that part of the world (Ghana) that has not known much freedom, and I can say without any reservation that it is terrible to live in an authoritarian environment. But it is equally terrible to live in a society with unrestrained freedom. A society in which everyone strives toward the fullest expression of their freedom without any self-restraint can be just as dangerous as a society without any freedom. As I will show in this chapter, how Americans have used their freedoms demonstrates the "inequality between the freedom for good deeds and the freedom for evil deeds." In the United States, too much freedom without restraint and responsibility has provided a license for many Americans to indulge in excesses and has furthered many antisocial behaviors, such as crime and violence. While freedom by itself may not lead to violence or the commission of crimes, it is quite obvious that some of the individual freedoms available in a democratic society may promote violence and criminal acts.

This is particularly the case where society has not provided adequate defenses against the destructive and irresponsible use of freedom. It appears that America has not made adequate and effectively enforced provision for "the abyss of human decadence, for example against the misuse of liberty for moral violence against young people, such as motion pictures full of pornography, crime and horror.[2] This is all considered to be part of freedom and to be counterbalanced, in theory, by the young people's right not to look and not to accept."[3] This implies that freedom itself must be defended from abuse, but American numerous freedoms have shown their acute inability to defend themselves against the "corrosion of evil." In America's pluralistic society, there is no agreement on what is truth. Thus clear thinking about moral truth "founders on the rocks of relativism. Individualism the nemesis of conformity, has become the basis for most ethical and moral judgements." Although many

Americans may view individualism and the pursuit of self-interest as ideals in and of themselves, the U.S. Constitution actually provides a legalistic basis for their accomplishment. In other words, there is a legal enforcement of what is perceived as American values. Simply stated, freedom promotes individualism and the pursuit of self interest. Preoccupation with self-interest can invariably lead to disregard for the interests of others. For this reason, society cannot live only by legalistic freedoms, without an attendant significant antisocial behavior.

Alexis de Tocqueville during his travels throughout the United States in the 1830s observed that America's democracy had loosened social ties and that outside the family order, equality had tended to isolate people and to make them selfish. He went on to say that this could lead to complete conformity or, at the extreme, to "unrestrained individualism."[4]

Freedom to bear arms, for example, means easy accessibility to a gun. Not surprisingly, guns are the major weapons of choice for committing crime in the United States. Freedom of movement may lead to the lack of any significant long-term attachment and commitment to any particular place or community. Tocqueville was struck by the Americans' lack of attachment to anything and observed, "The American has no time to tie himself to anything. He grows accustomed only to change . . . and regards it as a natural state of man."[5] This may lead to the reduction of any strong sense of responsibility to any particular place or community, lack of support to a community, and possibly lack of restraint when perpetrating any antisocial behavior.

But there are several other countries with at least as much freedom guaranteed under their constitution as the United States, countries such as Great Britain, the Scandinavian countries, and Switzerland, where freedom has not led to so much antisocial behavior.

Perhaps the difference lies not only in the differences in the nature of the people in these countries, but also in the interpretation of their freedoms and their sense of social responsibility. Many Americans also interpret freedom to imply equal opportunity, fairness, and justice. For many of these individuals, equality of opportunity is sometimes viewed as synonymous with the ability to have everything someone else has, to be able to achieve what everybody else can achieve, and to overcome all sorts of barriers, restraints, and inadequacies. In simple terms, Americans want freedom without any restraint. This is perhaps one thing that every visitor instantly observes in the United States. Tocqueville also observed this in the United States and remarked, "here freedom is unrestrained."[6]

When all of the above freedoms (movement, speech, liberty, pursuit of happiness, to bear arms, equal opportunity, etc.) that individuals demand, and sometimes need to have in order to function in a pluralistic society, are brought to bear on society, they tend to increase the possibility for an American to commit a criminal act, or to use violence as a means to obtain what he or she sees as a right under the law, or what he or she sees as entitlement as a human being.

For example, the average American believes that he or she has not only the freedom, but also the right and equal opportunity to share in the material and economic abundance of the nation -- a right to attain the American dream. Of course, there is nothing inherently wrong with this desire, but in many cases this is a misconception.   Not all Americans have equal opportunity to attain the American dream.   Black Americans in particular, and women in general, are discriminated against to the extent that they have a much more difficult time attaining the dream.

For those to whom the dream is achievable to, a lot may be wrong with the means selected to achieve the ends. For example, many Americans deeply believe that their quest to attain this dream, nobody should stand in their way-- not state or federal government, not husband or children, not neighbor or friends, not mother or father, and indeed, not even themselves! Nothing can come between them and the consuming desire to succeed. They see no other acceptable alternative to success and other choice.

Meanwhile, society also expects them to succeed and, even more, to outperform their parents in the competition for material and economic success. After all, the American dream has always been that each generation could, if they worked hard, be better than the generation that preceded them. So one accepts this challenge and resolves to succeed at all cost. But the American dream cannot be viewed from only an economic perspective. It also has a social dimension, and its accomplishment has significant social effects.

The dream must be accomplished, and any stumbling block--social, economic, personal, or otherwise--must be overcome.   After all, Americans have also been conditioned by society to believe that, not only must they succeed, but also they have an equal chance, like everyone else, to succeed. They now see failure only as a refection of their own weakness and personal frailty.

They may very well also have been told that to succeed, they must be aggressive, assertive of their rights, be individualistic, and competitive. They accept these as the status quo and many times do not question any of them. Most likely, however, they may not have been told that this quest for personal achievement, and the attributes required to attain it, can at their extreme lead to lack of loyalty and superficial relationships, based purely on self-interest, greed, corruption, fraud, and indifference. Tocqueville wrote this of the United States in 1831:

We are certainly in another world. The profound   passion, the only one which profoundly stirs the human heart, the passion of all the days is the acquisition of riches . . . this thirst for riches . . . brings in its train many hardly honourable passions, such as cupidity, fraud, and bad faith.[7]

While this consuming desire to succeed may not be uniquely American, many societies, such as African societies, that place society's interests above individual interests tend to suppress these selfish instincts.   Americans instead place individual interests and rights above community interests and rights, and thus treasure individuality, which encourages the pursuit of individual selfish instincts. In the search for the American dream, everything must be interpreted as either success or failure. It is literally true that in the United States "everybody loves a winner." Loyalty, love, and attention belong only to the winner. The United States may perhaps be the only place in the world where a movie or a football star can make $1 million in one year and earn nothing the following year simply because the star is no longer "hot."

In the United States, you need to stay hot and ahead at all times. It appears that everything in this country is in a state of perpetual motion. Nothing seems to remain constant very long. "Fortune, and fame last for only a season, and reputations during the twinkle of an eye." As Vice President Walter Mondale remarked two years after his defeat for the presidency, "When you lose, they simply throw you over the edge of the cliff and it's over."

Indeed, "there appears to be an irresistible current that seems to sweep away everything in this country, and for many Americans, the only way to survive this current is to stay one step ahead of everyone, to keep in constant circulation, motion and in boiling agitation." Obviously, reaching and staying at the top cannot be accomplished without a great deal of pressure, frustration, and personal sacrifice.

Meanwhile, the average American preoccupied with the trappings of success and having "lost his traditional respect for the wisdom of the old, and his ancestors, and the culture of kindred nations, has little but abstractions and baseless utopias to compare himself with." The average American's expectation is extravagant and his optimism boundless. In time, the optimism becomes so blinding that it becomes impossible to distinguish images from realities. This eternal optimism furthers one's indulgence in extravagant expectations. As a result, Americans according to Boorstin: Expect new heroes every season, a literary masterpiece every month, a dramatic spectacular every week, and a rare sensation every night . . . We expect everything and anything. We expect the contradictory and the impossible. We expect compact cars which are spacious; luxurious cars which are economical. We expect to be rich and charitable, powerful and merciful, active and reflective, kind and competitive. . . . We expect to eat and stay thin.[8] Many Americans in their boundless optimism have become so accustomed to illusions that they mistake them for reality.

However, "when the struggle for success, achievement, and the American dream turns out to be dead ends, or when competition becomes unbearable and the pressure point begins to explode, when failure becomes eminent and inevitable, or indeed, when the victory of success becomes too sweet, and the desire to stay on top too consuming, Americans in their great numbers begin to seek escape routes. Many find their refuge in drugs, crime, and violence, divorce, child abuse, and many antisocial behaviors.

As a result, in America today a serious crime is committed every 3.5

seconds, robbery is reported every 83 seconds, and a murder is committed every 27 minutes. There is one divorce for every 1.8 marriages, and over 1 million children a year are involved in divorce cases. Today, more than 13 million American children under the age of eighteen have one or both parents living away from them.[9] Cases of the battered child have been increasing at an alarming rate in America over the last few years. Reports of child abuse soared from 600,000 in 1979 to 2.4 million in 1989. In Los Angeles, the number of drug-exposed babies entering the foster care system rose 453 percent between 1984 and 1987.[10]

Crime is so pervasive in America that no city, state, or village is spared from its impact. Washington D.C., the nation's capital, has recently been given the dubious distinction of the title, the "crime capital of the world," and residents, visitors, and sightseers to the capital are robbed, mugged, and beaten only a few blocks from the White House. Both political leaders and aspirants have been shot and killed on the American streets and hotels, and many can't appear in public without an army of security men. Recently, the White House has become a fortress.

I am rather amazed at the American media's coverage and obsession with overseas violence when so much of it is going on in American homes and streets. In 1986, a record number of Americans stayed away from Europe and overseas generally because there allegedly were too many incidents of terrorist activities there. But regardless of increased terrorist activity abroad, Americans know very well that there are more terroristic activities in the United States at any point in time than perhaps anywhere in Europe.

In 1985, for example, 6.5 million Americans visited Europe. Of this total only 10 died from terrorist incidents. That is 1 out of every 650,000 American visitors died in a terrorist incident per year in Europe. The probability of being killed in America is 52 times this number. In Britain, for example, 1.3 per 100,000 are murdered compared to 10 per 100,000 in the United States. In 1986, between January and April, 5 Americans were killed in Europe in terrorist incidents, during the same period, 462 people were murdered in New York city alone. Data released in September 1993 by the Federal Bureau of Investigation (FBI) show that one murder is committed per day in Washington, D.C., alone.

If all the crimes that take place in American homes and streets were occurring in some developing country, that country would simply be classified as barbaric and uncivilized. In 1990 alone, more than 6 million American were the victims of violent crimes.[11]

Reflecting soberly on the crime situation in the United States at an anticrime conference in 1991, President Bush stated, "During the first three days of the ground offensive, more Americans were killed in some American cities than at the entire Kuwaiti front. Think of it--one of our brave National Guardsmen may have actually been safer in the midst of the largest armored offensive in history than he would have been on the streets of his hometown."[12]

Today more than one of every six hundred Americans is in prison. Only

South Africa at the peak of it apartheid policy and the Soviet Union in the era of communism had a greater percentage locked up. In the United States, civilized men and women are doing primitive things to each other! But these Americans are not "savages from Africa"; rather, they are the so-called civilized people from the West.

Americans may deplore, and in fact fear, violence, but they do not appear to be deeply shocked by it. They have a culture of violence and seem to accept violence as a normal part of life's events. They do not gather to protest, oppose, or seek to control it. During his tenure President Bush made another connection between crime and America's recent victory over Iraq. His remarks again underscored America's ambivalence in fighting crime. He stated: "The kind of moral force and national will that freed Kuwait City from abuse can free America's cities from crime."[13]

Noam Chomsky, a scholar and linguist, has written that "America is without parallel a source of violence." In 1960, the black radical H. Rap Brown noted that violence is "as American as cherry pie." Violence is endemic in America, among other reasons, because many Americans tend to be very emotional compared to, say, Africans who tend to suppress their emotions. And it appears that many aspects of American life have either overt or veiled references to violence.

American entertainment, writings, and sports are all suffused with an intolerable amount of violence. Even at a time when there has been an explosion of violence in the United States, American books and television programs are still glorifying violence as if it were meant to be cultivated as part of the mainstream American culture.

Many of America's recent national icons have tended to be men who excel at violence, especially John Wayne and Clint Eastwood. In addition, many Americans appear to derive enjoyment from acts of violence; perhaps they derive a sense of superiority from a show of force and conquest. For example, when President Clinton ordered a retaliatory air strike on Baghdad because of an alleged plot against President Bush, Clinton's popularity ratings immediately took a leap, just as Bush's had when, as president, he ordered the Gulf War in which an estimated one hundred thousand Iraqi civilians were killed by bombs and missiles.[14] The terrible sights and sounds of American missiles over Baghdad were shown on American television and were enjoyed by many Americans as if they were fourth of July fireworks. As an American said, "The culture of aggression shows up in our speech, our plays, and our entertainment. It's better than hip, it's commercial."[15]

Today America's culture of violence is a legacy that is been passed on from the older to the younger generation. Howard Synder of the National Center for Juvenile Justice states that in the last five years, the number of murders committed by youths under eighteen years has skyrocketed by 85 percent.[16] FBI figures also show that, while arrests for adult sex offenders rose by 3 percent between 1990 and 1991, the increase was three times as high for adolescents.[17]

U.S. Attorney General Janet Reno concedes that youth violence is the "greatest single crime problem in America today."[18]

The FBI's Uniform Crime Report released in 1993 shows that of those arrested between 1987 and 1992 for the most violent crimes, 29 percent were under the age of eighteen. A study by Northwestern University in 1992 also showed that between 1985 and 1991, the number of seventeen year olds arrested for murder increased by 121 percent, the number of sixteen year olds by 185 percent, and the number of fifteen year olds by 217 percent. For boys twelve years and under, it was over 100 percent. [19] American youths are not only perpetrators of crime, but they are also victims of crime. Every forty seven seconds, a child is abused or neglected, and every thirty six minutes, a child is killed or injured by a gun. The FBI data shows that more than 2,200 murder victims in 1991 were under eighteen--an average of more than six young people killed every day in the United States. The Justice Department estimates that each year nearly 1 million young people between the ages of twelve and nineteen are raped, robbed, or assaulted, often by their peers.[20]

The increase in crime among American youths is attributable to several reasons, including "neglect and abuse by parents; witnessing of violence at an early age on the street or in the house, living in a culture that glamorizes youth violence in decades of movies *A Clockwork Orange* to *Menace II Society*; and the continuing mystery of evil." But above all, the greatest contributor to crime is the widespread availability of guns in American society. In a Harvard School Public Health Survey released late July 1993, 59 percent of children in the sixth through twelfth grade said they "could get a hand gun if they wanted one."[21]

Another popular refuge for Americans when the going gets tough (and an escape is necessary) is alcohol. The desire to take refuge in alcohol is so great that today there are over 25 million alcoholics in the United States.[22] Most of these alcoholics attribute their alcoholism to their inability to cope with societal pressures or standards for success that they have unquestionably accepted and attempted to live up to -- a good job, a stable and loving family, a house with two cars parked in the garage, as well as a good bank account. And yes, there are those who have been squeezed out of the American dream who in their frustration and alienation also resort to alcoholism in large numbers.

Similarly, the 43 million Americans who are regular users of marijuana, the 5 million users of cocaine, and the one-half million heroin addicts generally attribute their drug dependency to their inability to meet the extravagant expectations placed on them by society. Today, the over $70 billion American alcohol industry is having a difficult time coping with the ever increasing demand even though alcoholism has become a national problem, with fatal results and serious economic implications. In America today, drunkenness is the cause for 30 to 50 percent of all traffic deaths, 45 percent of all fatal falls, 87 percent of murders, 72 percent of assaults, and 50 percent of rapes.[23]

A study of teenage alcoholism in the United States showed that 70 percent of Georgia's eight graders (fourteen year olds) had used alcohol in great quantities and that one of every five freshmen at the University of Minnesota admitted to being heavy drinkers. This study also concluded that their findings were not unique and that similar results were likely throughout the country. The study further indicated that there is a significant link between television advertisement and entertainment programs that seek to portray drinking as macho, cute, and acceptable social behavior and the increasing alcoholic use among young people in the United States. The study concluded on a less than optimistic note, stating that the trend toward teenage alcoholism is expected to increase in the United States. Thus, television appears to help prepare kids for alcoholism, and societal pressures and unfulfilled expectations really trigger alcoholism in adult Americans.

Many of the things that Americans do to make life more interesting, more exciting, more vivid, and more promising, in many cases produce an unintended negative opposite result. In the extravagance of their expectations and increasing economic and technological powers, many "Americans have transformed elusive dreams into graspable images in which they can all fit." Drug addiction illustrates this point best. Many Americans who take drugs do so, they would argue, to get "high", to be on top of the world, and to enlarge their life's experiences. In this quest, however, many people almost always hurt not only themselves, but also their loved ones.

Granted, Americans who take drugs obviously love their drugs, but many of them also love and care very much about their families, especially their children. Nonetheless, it is estimated that some of the 5 million Americans who use cocaine regularly may be inadvertently passing their addiction to their unborn children. The repulsive "Cocaine kids," a revelation that started appearing in the news only about ten years ago, have now become increasingly commonplace. As stated previously, the number of drug-exposed babies entering the foster care system rose by 453 percent between 1984 and 1987. Today, they make up more than 60 percent of all drug-affected babies born to addicts participating in a program at Northwestern Memorial Hospital in Chicago. In Los Angeles, they account for more than one-half of the drug-associated births reported to the department of children's services. In a recent study, it was found that cocaine users have an extraordinarily high incidence of miscarriage (38%) and a higher than normal rate of premature labor.

Alcoholism and illegal drugs have become so pervasive in the United States that they affect people in almost all industries and institutions. For many Americans drugs have become a daily companion -- both blue-and white-collar workers alike. Drug use at the workplace is sapping energy and destroying the reliability of the American labor force even as foreign competition intensifies. The costs of drug abuse on the job are staggering. The consequences range from accidents and injuries to theft and poor worker judgment.

According to the North Carolina based Research Triangle Institute, drug abuse cost the U.S. economy over of $117 billion in 1983 alone. It is now estimated at more than $200 billion. More than fifty train accidents have been attributed to drug or alcohol-impaired workers since 1975. The National Transportation Safety Board attributed a fatal 1983 air accident to illegal drug abuse. When two crewmen died in an incident where a cargo flight crash-landed at Newark International Airport in 1986, their autopsies revealed that the pilot had been smoking marijuana, possibly while flying.[24]

Illicit drugs have made their way to every sector and segment of American society. Today, nothing appears sacrosanct to the reach of drugs in the United States. Even the proud all-American space program has not been spared from its reach. Dr. Howard Frankel, the former medical director of Rockwell's Space Shuttle Division from 1981 to 1983, says that he treated employees who were hallucinating on the job. He states that as many as 20 to 25 percent of the employees were drug abusers. [25]

It is very difficult to find any aspect of American life, culture, or activity that is free from the influence of drug and alcoholism today. Drug use is pervasive in professional sports, in the movie and entertainment industries, as well as in American schools, colleges, and universities.

But there are other problems that the desire to attain the American dream and its consequences have bequeathed to the American society. In the desperate search for the American dream, greed, dishonesty, corruption, and bribery become not only useful "assets" but important traits to possess. After all, the American dream revolves mainly around material and economic success. And with the American philosophy seemingly without absolutes in right and wrong, with only strong emphasis on entrepreneurial individualism, success, achievement, freedom, and liberty, it is not surprising that many Americans would do anything--kill, cheat, lie, and even compromise U.S. national security concerns--just to attain economic and material success. For example, in the 1980s at the time when President Reagan was telling Americans, "There is a rebirth of patriotism. There is a pride in this country that is so evident," some Americans were aggressively pursuing the American dream by selling American national security secrets and information to largely American adversaries.[26] To many Americans, when it comes to the "almighty dollar," nothing can be allowed to stand in the way.

Many visitors to this country have sometimes wondered whether when Americans inscribed "In God we trust" on their currency they did not mean it literally? Here, in the United States, as well as abroad, the United States dollar has become a god with fervent and devout followers. As people throughout history fought, cheated, lied, and killed in the name of God, so likewise the Americans and the rest of the world today do no less in the name of the "almighty dollar."

Between 1984 and 1986, for example, more than twenty people were arrested for selling high-level national security secrets to Eastern Block countries, China, and Israel. As the FBI director, William Webster, had to confess at the time, "We have more people charged with espionage right now than ever before in our history."[27]

As can be expected, in many of the espionage cases, the spies confessed that money was the prime motive for their actions.[28] It is not at all surprising, as the motive of these Americans shows, that a people so obsessed with materialism should subscribe to the principle that the end justifies the means. These individuals are therefore willing to compromise and to use all means, including dishonesty, to attain their materialistic ends. Monetary rewards that some of the spies received are as follows;

-Ronald Pelton made $25,000 for selling military secrets to the Soviet Union
-Jonathan Pollard received $50,000 for selling military secrets to Israel
-Larry Wu-Tai Chin, a Central Intelligence Agency (CIA) agent reaped $140,000 for selling military secrets to China
-Richard Miller was paid $65,000 for the sale of military information to the Soviet Union
-Three members of the John Walker family received over $332,000 for selling military secrets to the Soviet Union
-A Northrop engineer, Thomas Cavanaugh, received $55,000 from the Russians for providing information about the American Stealth Bomber technology.[29]

In many of these cases, the monetary rewards were insignificant relative to the potential damage that the activities of these spies could inflict on national security. However, as I stated earlier, when the desire to succeed becomes an obsession, reason, as well as patriotism, tends to be sacrificed for material and economic purposes.

But the real issue is this: Having granted practically all its citizens the desired freedoms and access to material goods in "such quantity as to theoretically guarantee the achievement of happiness, "having imbued in its citizens the constant desire to have still more things and a still better life, a life better than their fathers, and one that their grandfathers could not even dream about, can the United States expect its citizens to "renounce all these in defense of any common good, and particularly, a nebulous common good like national security," an American writer asks.

The painful truth is that spying for money is so embarrassing for this country where the flag means so much that until 1975, the Justice Department gave the Central Intelligence Agency (CIA) discretion to conceal crimes by its own agents. Even as I write this book, no one seems to know for sure how many espionage cases there have been and how many have been deliberately kept secret to avoid embarrassing the nation.

Be that as it may, what is worse--a few individuals selling national security secrets to support their life- styles in the spirit of the American dream, or giant multimillion defense contractors overcharging, overbilling, filing false claims, or out and out stealing dollars intended for national security of which they are a part?

During President Reagan's first term in office, Congress heeded his call to rearm America by giving the Pentagon $1.1 trillion to spend, a 36 percent real increase over the previous year's budget. But what came out of these outlays may not have been significant increases or improvement in America's military readiness, but $436 hammers, $7,600 coffee makers, $6,400 toilet seat covers, $180 flashlights, and $620 ash trays.[30]

Corruption in defense procurement and contract awards in this country would spark off military coups d'etat in any African country and would bring the masses onto the streets to demonstrate against the government, even at the risk of being shot at mercilessly. Cases of corruption are well documented, yet they elicit no national outcry or any organized effort to halt it. For example, a top Pentagon official negotiates a settlement with a shipbuilder that requires that the government pay nearly $500 million to the shipbuilder.[31] After quitting his government job a few months later, he ends up as a paid consultant to the same shipbuilder. An obvious conflict of interest? No. Not under the United States laws prevailing at that time. Cases such as these are more widespread than anyone could conceivably expect in the United States, an open society, where the press is quite vigilant.

It is estimated that in the early 1980s alone, during the great American defense buildup, over three thousand senior military and civilian defense department officials took jobs with major defense contractors after quitting their jobs in government. In all cases, these officials joined companies with which they had negotiated government contracts while they served in government. Air Force whistle-blower, Ompal Chauhan, warned against "a type of cultural conditioning in which a typical Pentagon manager thinks more about his future employer than his current one. Loyalties become confused."

Among the most widely publicized revolving-door cases is that of former Navy Secretary Edward Hildago and General Dynamics, the largest defense contractor for the United States government. In 1978, Hildago negotiated a settlement with General Dynamics for over $843 million in claims filed against the government for cost overruns. Working as the lead U.S. government negotiator, Hildago negotiated an agreement that required the United States Navy to pay General Dynamics $484 million. Less than eleven months after leaving the Pentagon in 1981, Hildago was retained as a consultant for General Dynamics and was paid $66,000.

The same greed that motivates the average American in his search for the American dream propels American corporations to steal and cheat, even if it means subverting national security. Incidentally, General Dynamics perhaps benefited more than any U.S. defense contractor from the Reagan defense buildup. With 1984 profit in excess of $384 million, one would expect that such a company would feel quite content. But this is far from the case. In the same year when it earned these excess profits, it charged the government as overhead cost $14,975 for a party held at a suburban Washington country club and baby-sitting expenses of its officials.[32] In 1982 alone, such dubious billings by General Dynamics amounted to $182 million.

Questionable entertainment and gifts equally abound in the billings to the

Defense Department which are generally paid from the taxes of low- and middle-income taxpayers, not from the rich corporations or rich individuals. For example, in 1982, General Dynamics headquarters maintained a $1.24 million account, which was against government rules, to entertain Pentagon officials. Gifts also flow freely.

Cases of corruption just as blatant as that of General Dynamics have been uncovered among top defense contractors such as the LTV Corporation, General Electric, and Boeing. Corruption in the Defense Department has been covered up for a long period of time in the fear that such revelations may arouse public indignation and hurt defense appropriations. However, it has now reached a point that it can no longer be concealed. For example, about eight years ago, defense engineer Ralph Applegate was dismissed for disclosing that the armed services were paying $1,130 apiece for piston rings for which civilian buyers were paying only $100.

Slowly but increasingly, the American public has become incensed over the corruption and waste in the Defense Department, and the case such as above would now be welcome and would not result in a loss of a job. Public outrage against corruption and waste in the Defense Department is justified given the tremendous amount of money allocated to defense at the same time social programs are being cut. For example, in 1991 alone the U.S. defense budget exceeded $300 billion. At the same time the budget deficits have been increasing at a phenomenal rate. It makes sense that as resources have become increasingly scarce, efficiency in public expenditure and effective resource use have become important goals.

But why is there so much corruption in the defense contracts? The answer is simple. Many experts in defense contracting attribute this level of corruption to the lack of competitive bidding. Less than 10 percent of all defense contracts for weapons are subject to stringent competitive bidding. In fact, the Defense Science Board has said that competition might lower costs by as much as 20 percent on the average contract. If this is true, why is there so little competitive bidding in U.S. defense contracting then? The truth is that competitive bidding will completely upset the delicate military-industrial balance that has been forged between defense contractors and the military. This symbiotic relationship provides an opportunity for each organization to support each other in their battles with Congress and the American public. The fear is that competitive bidding will destroy the patronage system that has been designed to maintain economic and political power in the hands of the patriarchal Euro-American ruling elite class. In simple everyday language, you can call it political corruption (see Chapter 5).

The American family has also paid a great price for economic and technological success. The technological breakthroughs that have allowed mass production of automobiles has meant increased mobility for American children, allowing them to escape their parents' watchful eyes. Moreover, the development of the birth control pill has allowed sexual experimentation and eliminated many of the social stigmas against premarital sex. The development of modern household appliances and conveniences has reduced the drudgery of home-making for many women, and has freed up many housekeeping hours.

The feminist movement has also helped liberated women from seeing themselves as good only for having children, taking care of their husbands, and maintaining and cleaning house. For many women, who have been freed up from housekeeping, either due to technological developments or the feminist movement, the emotional, psychological, and economic need to work outside the home has been great. Increasingly, therefore, women have sought gainful employment outside the home. In many families in the United States today, it is the rule rather than the exception that both parents have jobs outside the family. While there is significant disagreement as to the effect of parents being increasingly unavailable for their children, there are some basic points of agreement. For the children as well as for the parents, having only one parent working outside the home is better than having both working outside the home. This is particularly the case since it is now estimated that parents are spending more time at work than at home and that the impact of television and VCR on children is not being mitigated by a caring parent.

Stephen Klineberg, a professor of sociology at Rice University, estimates that the parent is working 50 or 60 hours a week and is increasingly unavailable when the children return from school. For example, "in 1974, for the first time, 50 percent of American children had nobody at home when school let out at 3 o'clock. Now, it's closer to 80 percent, but schools still kick kids out at 3."[33]

For some of these women who have not been able to make any productive use of their freed-up time, it has sometimes meant an urge to seek some exciting outlet from the boredom at home. In some cases they resort to extramarital sexual activities. Some people in the United States believe that the price that the American family has had to pay for its technological progress, economic success, the success of the feminist movement, and the changes in the structure and nature of the family, has been fractured families, child abuse, infidelity, teenage suicide, drug abuse, illegitimate births, breakdown of the sense of family, stress, lack of attention, and a sense of each for oneself, and a God-helps-us-all attitude.

To expand further on this matter, let us look at the impact of economic success on the American family. At the same time that technological advances were reducing household chores, the economy was expanding in leaps and bounds and thus providing new employment opportunities for women to spend their freed-up time as well as meeting their own emotional or psychological need to work. The result has been a dramatic participation of women in the labor force and economy. However, the addition of increasing numbers of women, especially married women, to the labor force has had a profound effect on American family life. In 1948, 18 percent of American mothers worked outside the home, in 1971, this figure jumped to 43 percent, and in 1993, to over 50 percent.

As more and more women worked outside the home, they became more and more independent, both economically and socially. As working women sought to mediate the contradictory demands of professional and traditional female responsibilities and human relationships, as they tried "to have it all," they became much more exposed to the business pressures and stresses that their husbands had been exposed to for years, which in many cases have been different from the stresses involved in housekeeping and motherhood. Many women, like men, are turning to drugs to deal with the stress and depression. Dr. Beatrice Rouse, an epidemiologist with the National Institute on Drug Abuse, says that cocaine use among women increased from 6.4 percent in 1979 to 9.3 percent in 1982. The California State Department of Alcohol and Drug Programs reports that the number of women checking into cocaine treatment centers jumped 73 percent between 1982 and 1984. For the working women in the United States, it is a constant, ongoing process of internalizing the cultural contradictions of gender, mediating opposing cultural demands, and dealing with nagging problems of competency and self-esteem.

The increasing stress and pressures that working women are exposed to, combined with the changing nature of American society, the glorification of violence, the economic difficulties of taking care of a family, the weakening extended family support network--all have contributed to the increased marital stress, the high divorce rate, child abuse cases, infidelity, alcoholism, drug dependency and addiction, violence in the home, high teenage suicide, and the high rate of homicide. (These problems that plague the modern American family are discussed extensively in the next chapter.)

If attaining a piece of the American dream was tough, trying to sustain the dream is even harder. Sustaining the dream requires as much hard work as the initial quest for the dream. One has to be on his toes constantly and to stay one step above the crowd, and herein enter the pressures and the stress.

Pressures and stress in American society are enormous, as carefully articulated in a recent article in an American news magazine, "The sense of panic over a deadline, a tight plane connection, a reckless driver at your tail, an upcoming review, presentations and evaluations are only a few of the many things that can set the heart racing, the teeth gritting, and the cold sweat streaming down in rapid succession."

In the past thirty years, doctors and health officials have come to recognize the heavy toll that stress is taking on America's well-being. According to the American Academy of Family Physicians, two-thirds of office visits to family doctors are prompted by stress-related symptoms. At the same time, industry leaders have become incensed by the increasing cost of such symptoms in absenteeism, company medical expenses, and lost productivity. Based on national samples, these costs have been estimated at $50 billion to $75 billion a year, or more than $750 per worker.

Stress is now a major contributor either directly or indirectly to coronary heart disease, cancer, lung ailments, accidental injuries, cirrhosis of the liver, and suicide, six of the leading causes of death in the United States. It is disturbing to know that three of the most popular drugs in this country today are used to treat stress-related illness: ulcer medication (tagament), a hypertension drug (Inderal), and a tranquilizer (valium).[34] Dr. Joe Elkes, director of the behavioral medicine program at the University of Louisville, concludes, "Our mode of life itself, the way we live, is emerging as today's principal cause of illness."[35]

What is it about the American way of life that causes so much stress-related illness? Do Americans have more stress today than ever? Are Americans exposed to more stress than are peoples from other countries? No one seems to know all the answers to these questions. But it is true that America's advances in science and technology, living standards, and changing American lifestyles have all contributed in great measure to the epidemic of stress in America today. Indeed, says Harvard University's Professor Benson, "We live in a world of uncertainties, everything from nuclear threat, to job insecurity to the near assassination of the President, to the lacing of medicines with poisons."[36] These, according to many experts, are in a large measure responsible for the pervasiveness of stress in the United States.

Although stress is a worldwide problem that may take the form of an occasional calamity, in the United States stress has become a permanent feature of life. It is now "a chronic relentless psychosocial situation," says Dr. Paul Rosch, director of the American Institute of Stress in Yonkers, New York. If stress poses health and medical problems for Americans, so do overweight and excess fat.

The United States produces more food on a per capita basis than any country in the world. The less than 3 percent of Americans who are engaged in agriculture are able to feed the nation as well as one-third of the world's food needs. However, as America feeds the world, it feeds itself even more generously. Food is in plentiful supply in America. The average person spends less per capita income on food than perhaps anyone anywhere in the world. For these reasons, Americans are always on the lookout for an occasion to stuff themselves. They get their major break in November every year on a day that many Americans have designated as the national day of feasting, the traditional Thanksgiving day. Thanksgiving day is an occasion that many Americans choose ostensibly to thank God for the bounty and the sustenance of the land.

On this day, Americans get up early and start to prepare their feasts. By 2 p.m., most families are "ready to now stuff themselves, having first stuffed their turkeys. With their well-baked, juicy turkeys, cranberry sauces, rolls, stuffing, and butter and other thanksgiving dinner paraphernalia, they will stuff themselves and wash them down with their caffeine laced coffee." This is repeated in a few weeks when they again sit down for their Christmas and New Year's dinners, not counting the various all-night dinner parties in between. Many believe that the American's appetite for food has contributed to their perceived excess weight. Nearly 90 percent of Americans think they that they weigh too much, according to a survey conducted in April 1985 by *Better Homes and Gardens*. More than 35 percent of the Americans surveyed indicated that they want to lose at least 15 pounds.

According to another survey by MRCA, a market research firm in Northbrook, Illinois, about 30 percent of American women and 16 percent of American men were on diets in 1984; it is estimated at over 30 percent in 1993. Another research study published by the University of California, San Francisco, in February 1986, showed that four-fifths of the girls in the fourth grade in California were dieting. Similarly, a poll conducted by Gallup and released in November 1985 showed that 31 percent of American women between the ages of nineteen and thirty-nine diet at least once a month. In 1993, 23 percent of children in the United States were considered obese.[37] While dieting per se does not imply an overweight condition, many respondents were doing so to lose weight. What is wrong with being overweight? What health risks does it involve, and how much are Americans willing to pay to stay slim?

Not only is being overweight a major source of many health-related problems, but it is an expensive disease. In the battle to combat their bulges, Americans spent about $5 billion in 1985; today the figure has more than doubled. Now they buy some $300 million worth of over-the-counter diet drugs containing caffeine and amphetamine-related compounds and pay out millions more for other "off-the-wall" remedies like kelp and grapefruit extracts. Sales of low-calorie frozen foods, have risen by more than 20 percent annually for the past several years, according to Pathmark, one of the largest food chains in America.

Determined to sweat off the excess fat, many overweight Americans are joining health clubs and spas. It is estimated that at least 2 million people have joined self-help groups like Weight Watchers, or TOPS (Take Off Pounds Sensibly); others visit diet doctors and nutrition specialists.

However determined and sustained these efforts are, the only guaranteed result for many of these people are much smaller and thinner wallets. Just as quickly as they shed off the excess fat, they turn around and put them back on one way or the other. And why? Americans love their juicy hamburgers, steak, and their rich, creamy desserts. Says Dr. John McCall, an endocrinologist in La Jolla, California, with regard to how quickly Americans tend to put back any weight they lose: "The statistics are horrible. It is like treating cancer." Indeed, studies have shown that at least two-thirds of those who lose weight *will* put it back on again.

If many Americans are concerned about what excess fat does to their appearance, they are equally concerned about the effect of excess fat on their health. One major effect of being obese is extra health risk and premature death. Among the dangers associated with excess weight are high blood pressure, heart disease, diabetes, gallstones, respiratory disorders, and degenerative changes in joints, especially the hips and knees. For example, fat men have a higher incidence of certain cancers, including those of the colon, rectum, and prostate. Overweight women run a much higher risk of developing malignant tumors of the ovaries and the uterine lining and, after menopause, of the breasts. In 1978 Beverly Winikoff of the Rockefeller Foundation and the Senate Select Committee on Diet noted:

Over 70 percent of all deaths in the United States in 1973 were caused by diseases linked to the consumption of our diet, including high levels of fat, sugar and salt. The leading causes of death, heart disease, stroke are related to the types of food we eat and over eat.[38]

Studies also show that mortality rates are 20 to 40 percent higher among overweight persons, and that overweight persons are more likely to succumb to heart disease, stroke, and diabetes.[39]

A panel of doctors and nutritionists meeting a few years ago at the National Institutes of Health concluded that more than 15.4 million American men (24.2 percent) and 18.6 million women (27.1 percent) between the ages of twenty and seventy-four fit the panel's description of clinical obesity. With these figures, it is not surprising that the United States already ranks as the world's fattest! "Europeans visit Disneyland and go back home thinking we all weigh 250 pounds," observes cardiologist John Farquhar of the Stanford University Medical Center.

While there is some disagreement in the scientific community as to whether all obesity may be due to food intake, there is a lot of agreement about the cultural influence and the role it plays in obesity. For example, researchers like to point to the Japanese who have a low rate of obesity in their native land, but become progressively heavier as they move east to Hawaii and then to the U.S. mainland. Many experts put the blame squarely on the American diet, the abundance of food in America, and the American eating habits. "The kinds of food people eat, high in fat and sugar, and low in nutrients and fiber, are what predispose people to obesity in this country," says nutritionist Marion Nestle of the Medical School of the University of California in San Francisco.

Food is abundantly available in America at all hours. It is easily available in the around-the clock restaurants, grocery stores, at fast-food stores, and through home delivery food services. All these opportunities increase the accessibility to food. But even more, "The American refrigerator is bulging with food," notes Dr. Theodore Van Itallie, of the Obesity Research Center at St Luke's Roosevelt Hospital in New York city. It is the American culture of eating at any time and anywhere that contributes to this problem. Many of us, as visitors to the United States, are shocked to see well-dressed men and women eating in the streets and chatting away. In many cultures around the world, this shows a basic lack of etiquette. In America on the other hand, says Dr. Van Itallie, "It is the American habit to eat from that refrigerator at all times of day" that may be most responsible for America's bulges.

Another great price that America has paid for its high standard of living, and its economic and material successes has been the imprisonment of many Americans in a state of mind that focuses on the present and is dominated by self-adulation, self-indulgence, and apathy. The words of lamentation spoken by a Roman senator for his country are very apt for the American situation today, "I fear for our nation . . . We have grown weak from too much affluence and too little adversity."

Many Americans tend to think of themselves as the beginning and the end of the world. They have become so obsessed with themselves, with their material affluence, and with where they are now that often they tend even to forget where they came from and what has made their nation great.

In their self-content, many Americans have become apathetic, indifferent, and oblivious to their surroundings. (The effect of this attitude on the American political process is discussed in detail in chapter 4.) However, there is more than political cost to this apathy; socially, the cost has been prohibitive.

In the United States today, a person can be attacked in broad daylight, children may be abused next door, and a person may be robbed or injured on the street, without anybody trying to intervene to help. Everybody seems to be so busy minding their own business that nobody appears to have time for anyone else. Robert Bellah states that "American society is becoming very self-oriented; or very individualist-oriented: what's in it for me, how much do I get out of it, and am I getting everything I'm entitled to in my life? This way of thinking is tearing down a lot that is right about the country. People don't seem to look at the repercussions of their individual actions outside of themselves."[40]

Bellah further states, "Sometimes Americans make a rather sharp dichotomy between private and public life. Viewing one's primary task as 'finding oneself' in autonomous self-reliance, separating oneself not only from one's parents but also from those larger communities and traditions . . . Individualism of this sort often implies a negative view of public life."[41]

For these and other reasons, in the United States, there are no brothers' keepers. As someone also puts it, "Americans treasure their liberty and independence, their individuality, and their constant search to add to their grasp more houses, land, stocks, bonds, cars, personal luxuries, and conveniences" too much to allow themselves to be bothered with someone else's problems. They want to be left alone, they can't afford the time to be their brothers' keepers. In a recent survey, 72 percent of those interviewed did not know the people who lived next door to them, and two-thirds never gave time to community service.[42]

Thus as hedonistic pleasure-seeking people, "Americans have time for their ball games, movies, drugs, alcohol, parties, and vacations but they simply cannot find time for their own children, much less care about their neighbor's or the millions of children who are abused, raped, and battered each year." In America, it appears that everyone lives only to please himself and nobody else. Echoing this sentiment, the Uruguayan writer, Jose Enrique Rodo wrote of the United States, "The United States stands for progress and material achievements, but it is a barren spiritual landscape. Cultural primacy in this hemisphere belongs to the Latins, who may be materially poor but are spiritually rich. "[43]

Nevertheless, several civic and community organizations in the United States provide help to the poor, the elderly, abused children, the sick, and many disadvantaged and handicapped people. Obviously, however, more needs to be done. Similarly, it is common knowledge that the United States gives generously to victims of disaster throughout the world. However, in general, the high sense of civic and community responsibility that guided the United States at its beginnings, as well as the United States' acute sense of moral leadership and responsibility, seems to have disappeared.

But apathy and self-indulgence are not the only problems that are distorting America's sense of reality. As an American writer says of Americans,

Americans have gotten so accustomed to living in illusions that they mistake them for reality. In their success, and apathy, they have become too mollified to admit to even their most obvious failings. They refuse, for example to accept that they are the most violent civilization the world has ever seen, the most wasteful and greedy people on earth today, accounting for less than 10 percent of the world's population, but consuming more than 30 percent of the world's resources, that there are more alcoholics and drug addicts in the United states than perhaps, any nation on earth, that their children are rebellious, disrespectful, and that, it is only a pretense when they tell the rest of the world that theirs is a civil society in which public moralities stand for anything less than complacent self-deception.

Echoing the same sentiments, A. C. Townssend, in a recent newspaper article, wrote:

Why obscure the sour truth from ourselves that our national aims encompass little more than crude selfishness and shallow patriotic self-aggrandizement. . . Recognize what we are with our skyscrapers and shopping malls, our superhighways and ICBMs, our laboratories, universities and arsenals: We are savages with wealth and technology far exceeding our sense of responsibility for the welfare of Earthmother, the communities of the human race and the inheritance of our collective posterity.

In their sense of moral superiority over all other peoples, Americans demand of others what they cannot or would not do themselves. For example, they demand nuclear nonproliferation while they are the only country on earth that has ever used atomic bombs against humankind. Yet, in their eternal self-righteousness, the U.S. government argues to the rest of the world that Americans can continue to develop and maintain their nuclear arsenal because theirs is a democratic, civilized society where decisions are debated and well reflected upon. They are unlike leaders in the primitive Third World country, where a dictator may decide to unilaterally use the bomb. But if the United States is seriously committed to a nuclear-free world, it can demonstrate such a commitment by first destroying its own nuclear arsenal, and having done that, it will have the moral authority and the credibility to demand the same of others. The United States cannot credibly tell the rest of the world not to develop something that it believes is important to have and with which it has continued to dominate and blackmail the world.

The U.S. government also demands that developing countries preserve their environment after the United States has already devastated its own in order to achieve economic and technological superiority over the rest of the world.

Upon reflection, one cannot but feel that America's sense of self-righteousness is not only baseless but also mind-boggling. Many Americans were ostensibly outraged when they learned that the cutting down of the Amazon forest by Brazilians would adversely affect wheat production in the midwestern states of the United States. The United States promptly issued orders to Brazil to halt its forest-cutting activities (in its own country). In doing so, America completely disregarded Brazil's national economic interests, development agenda, and national sovereignty.

How would Americans like it if Brazilians were to issue orders for the United States to stop the construction of the Tennessee dam for some perceived environmental reasons? Over and over again, the rest of the world, particularly the peoples from the developing world, are forced to make sacrifices so that Americans can maintain their extravagant life-style. Obviously, for Americans to continue to consume more than 30 percent of the world's resources while constituting only less than 10 percent of the world's population means that the rest of the world will have to consume less.

The United States has similarly demanded that Colombia, Peru, and other Latin American countries stop the growing and export of drugs to the United States because these drugs kill Americans. Why should the primary responsibility for stopping drug consumption lie with of the producers of drugs, and not with the consumers? Is it these countries' fault that Americans consume more drugs than any other peoples in the rest of the world? Doesn't the United States have an equal, if not greater, responsibility to control Americans' appetite for drugs? Perhaps Americans must ask themselves, What is it about the American nature, the American culture, and the American life that pushes people to consume so much drugs?

Above all, I am not sure whether the United States would not have produced drugs just like the Colombians, Peruvians, and the rest of drug producers, if it had had the ability to do so. After all, the United States is one of the world's largest arms dealers which continues to ship arms to countries in Latin America, Africa, and Asia so that these mostly impoverished countries can not only spend their meager resources on arms, but also kill themselves. It is remarkable that in a world in which twenty thousand children die each day, we spent over $20 million daily on arms, most of them purchased by impoverished peoples of the world in countries where this genocide occurs.

These days many American political leaders talk about a new world order. It is argued that in this new world order, all nations, small and big, poor and rich, will be respected, and diplomacy rather than military might and blackmail will be the basis for the resolving of international conflicts. However, the actual results are different from the political rhetoric.

Not too long after President Bush praised the dawn of this new world order, he dispatched his troops in a sense of an enlightened self-interest to destroy Iraq. When it suited America's economic, political, and strategic self-interest, it invaded Panama, and in an unprecedented act of humiliation, brought Panama's head of state, General Noriega, to the United States to be tried as a common criminal, in an American court, by American law, where he was convicted and jailed in an American prison! All this took place just after the dawning of the new world order.

Immediately after the general was arrested and brought to the United States, I asked my students "How would you feel if an American president had been arrested by another country, no matter what his alleged offense?" The response from my students was rather unanimous -- impossible! "No country can arrest our president, no matter what he does against another country. We are Americans." Should I have been surprised? The answer is obvious.

Now returning to the discussion of apathy, I find that apathy does more than keep Americans preoccupied with themselves. It breeds ignorance not only about national issues but also international issues. When President Reagan's nominee for national security, William Clark, could not name the capital of Zimbabwe or the president of South Africa, many Americans were surprised that the president would consider such a nominee. I was not so much surprised as outraged.

I felt rather that it was more of an insult to the people of America for their president to consider such a candidate for such an important position. However, upon reflection, I felt neither surprise nor outrage. After all, many American are not very knowledgeable about the rest of the world. Indeed, Judge Clark was no more uninformed internationally than the average American, even though the average American does not get appointed the president's national security advisor.

The Americans' high level of ignorance and international incompetence is rather ironic. With the growth of instant worldwide communications and the pervasive role of television in daily American life, it would be natural to expect that American knowledge of international issues and events to be fairly extensive and accurate. However, public opinion surveys have consistently showed otherwise.

The results of a 1981 poll showed that a mere one in four Americans could give the location of El Salvador correctly, despite its daily coverage in the American news diet; fewer than four in ten Americans could name the two countries involved in the Strategic Arms Limitation Talks (SALT), which had been going on for a number of years; and less than half of the Americans surveyed knew that the United States rather than the Soviet Union was a member of NATO, an alliance of which the United States is the leader and the major economic supporter.[44]

The question may be asked, Why should a superpower bother to learn about people from the less developed countries (LDCs)? A simple answer may be that because knowledge is good, in and of itself. But a more important reason perhaps may be that enhancing the level of the United States' international competence has become important precisely because of the changed and increasingly interdependent nature of the world. Americans understand profits, business, and economics well, and therefore appeals to this would bring the message home clearly.

The need to understand the world around America is perhaps clearest on the economic front. Since 1960, the total value of the U.S. foreign trade has grown from less than 10 percent to over 25 percent of the gross national product (GNP); 20 percent of the United States' industrial output is for export; the jobs of one in six U.S. production workers are directly dependent on international trade; 40 percent of the United States' farmland produces for the export market; and about a third of U.S. corporate profits are generated from international activities. [45]

In short, the context in which America operated in the past has changed so that today more than ever before decisions made overseas affect the economic and social well-being of many Americans. For this reason, the United States can no longer afford to be ignorant of the rest of the world.

If Americans are uninformed about international issues and affairs, perhaps that can be understandable, but their knowledge of public issues in the United States itself is just as bad, if not worse. Social scientist John Nesbit characterizes the situation correctly when he observes, "We are drowning in information but starved for knowledge." (The effects of this ignorance on U.S. public policy and the American political system are discussed in Chapter 4.)

There is a saying that children are the living messages that we send to a time that we will not see. It is also a truism that if you want to get a glimpse of the future of any country or nation, then look at its youths. They will be the men and women of tomorrow. For this reason, I decided to examine what motivates the youth of America. As should be expected, the average American youth is highly influenced by technology and things technological in his attitudes and expectations. I believe that the kinds of people that American youths consider as their heroes may, more than anything, best reflect their values, attitudes, ambitions, hopes, dreams, and indeed their fears.

The impact of technological progress on the American way of life and the resultant material success were greatly manifested when 315 American youths ranging in age from 18 to 24 were asked to identify their heroes from a long list of people selected from all over the world. The survey commissioned by *U.S. News and World Report* and released in April 1985 showed that for American youths, heroes for the most part were television personalities, generally movie and entertainment stars. Of the ten heroes selected by the sample, seven were either movie stars or television entertainers. The three nontelevision personalities were President Reagan, Pope John Paul 11, and Mother Theresa.

The impact of television is so great that in America, today, celebrity is confused with heroism. Earlier, as Daniel Boorstin stated, "The hero was distinguished by his achievement; the celebrity by his image or trademark; the hero created himself; the celebrity is created by the media. The hero was a big man or woman; the celebrity is a big name." The media-created heroes selected by these young men and women show that today's young people clearly seek to pattern themselves after people who, for the most part, are "boundlessly rich or successful." They are in most cases not looking up to people who are selflessly serving the interests of society, humankind generally, or motivated by any noble cause.

The same search for and the preoccupation with success and materialism that motivate the adult American so motivate the youth in the United States today. Again, as Boorstin observed,

In this life of illusion and quasi illusion, the person with solid virtues who can be admired for something more substantial than his well-knownness often proves to be the unsung hero: the teacher, the nurse, the mother, the honest cop, the hard worker at lonely, under-paid unglamorous unpublicized jobs. Their virtues are not the product of our effort to fill our void.[46]

So what is wrong with young Americans seeking to replace heroes with celebrities? I think this is nothing more than the self-indulgence and obsession that I have talked about earlier. By their selection, it is clear that young Americans have tended to forget that these celebrities, as Boorstin called them, "are made to order, made by other people for specific economic and material gains." The real American hero, on the other hand, Boorstin says, "stood for outside standards, for lofty purposes." By selecting these stars and glorifying them, many of these young Americans are trying to have, as Boorstin states, "celebrities stand in for the heroes they no longer have, or refuse to acknowledge. They forget that the word 'celebrity' is nothing more than 'well-knownness.' This makes the celebrity a tautology and an obsession."[47]

Many Americans imitate these celebrities after casting them into a great mold of greatness, forgetting that they are nothing but a more publicized version of themselves. Therefore, in their fascination with these celebrities, manifested by their attempts to imitate them in dressing, speaking, "worshipping," thinking, and acting like them, Americans are simply imitating themselves. Boorstin observes, "By imitating a tautology, we ourselves become a tautology; standing for what we stand for, reaching to become more emphatically what we already are. . . We look for models, and we see our own image."[48]

Yes, the modern Americans have become captives of their own illusion and obsession. They have imprisoned themselves in their success, achievement, and progress. And they have had to pay a supreme price for the success and progress.

But if the kind of people that American youth selected as their heroes signals a troubled future for American youth, the socioeconomic future that many of these youth face is equally disturbing. In the United States today, nearly one in four American children under age six lives in poverty. Every 8 seconds of the school day, a child drops out of school; every 26 seconds, a child runs away from home; every 47 seconds a child is abused or neglected; every 67 seconds, a teenager has a baby; every 7 minutes, a child is arrested for a drug offense, every 36 minutes, a child is killed or injured by a gun, and reports of child abuse have soared from 600,000 in 1979 to 2-4 million in 1989.[49]

Today America's ideal of freedom, liberty, life, and the pursuit of happiness is being challenged in its practicality, if not in itself. As American freedom has turned against itself, the American century of material and economic freedom has also been its century of "criminal calamity." It has been argued that in a free society, the fullest freedom of expression for the individual may also serve the interest of society as a whole. As President Kennedy observed, "The rights of every man are diminished when the rights of one man are threatened."

My question is this: America, where are the rights of the 230 million Americans, when the rights of 20 million American blacks are trampled on? Where are the rights of Americans when in this civilized nation a serious crime is committed every 3.5 seconds, one robbery is reported every 83 seconds and one murder is reported every 27 minutes?

What price for success in a super-industrialized, prosperous nation, in which suicide is one of the leading causes of death, where one out of every five children born as recent as 1985 will have some form of cancer and one out of the five will die from it? What price for success if the superhighways turn out to be deathtraps, such that millions are killed each year in traffic accidents? What price for success when six of the leading causes of death in the United States are directly related to the pressures and stress that bring about the material success?

What kind of a success is it that results in 12 million alcoholics, a quarter of a million heroin addicts, 5 million cocaine addicts, 43 million marijuana addicts, and 25 million alcoholics?

What price success for the American citizen "who knows that at any point in time, the many alcoholics, rapists, murderers, street muggers, and the drug addicts are sharing the same streets, the same buses, the same schools, the same parks, and the same public facilities with her?"

Whether the issue is about stress at work, the risk of walking the street, enjoying a public park, or riding the bus, life in contemporary America is out of sync with what one would expect in a civilized and advanced society. Indeed, an appropriate question is, Can one live a rich private life in a state of siege?

America may have achieved tremendous material, economic, technological, military, and industrial success, but these have been attained at the greatest possible cost. Thus, the "obligation to endure" gives every American the right to ask the questions above, before America "staggers into the night of moral nothingness."

NOTES

1. Daniel J. Boorstin, *The Image* (New York: Harper & Row, 1961), p. lll.

2. Ronald Berman, et al., ed. *Solzhenitsyn at Harvard* (Washington, D.C.: Ethics and Public Policy Center, 1980), pp. 7 - 10.

3. Ibid.

4. John A. Garraty, *The American Nation* (New York: Harper & Row, 1983), Portfolio Three, p. 14.

5. Ibid., p. 9.

6. Ibid., p. 2.

7. Ibid., p. 3.

8. Boorstin, *The Image*, p. 4.

9. *The Rebirth of America* (Philadelphia: Arthur S. DeMoss Foundation, 1986), p. 76.

10. See *Time*, October 8, 1990, p. 46.

11. See *Wall Street Journal*, March 8, 1991, p. A10.

12. Ibid., p. A10.

13. Ibid., p. A10.

14. *Newsweek*, August 2, 1993, p. 45.

15. Ibid., p. 48.

16. *Newsweek*, July 19, 1993, p. 17.

17. Ibid.

18. *Newsweek*, August 2, 1993, p. 43.

19. *Wall Street Journal*, November 8, 1993, p. A14.

20. Ibid., p. 44.

21. Ibid., p. 43.

22. Joseph D. Beasley, *The Betrayal of Health* (New York: Random House, 1991), p. 164.

23. Ibid., p. 170.

24. *Time*, March 17, 1986, p. 53.

25. Ibid., p. 53.

26. *Time*, November 19, 1984, p. 52.

27. *Time*, April 29, 1985, p. 49, See also *U.S. News and World Report*, June 10, 1985, p. 34.

28. *U.S. News & World Report,* June 17, 1985, p. 21.

29. Ibid., pp. 20 - 34, See also *U.S. News & World Report*, June 17, 1985, pp. 21-22.

30. *U.S. News & World Report*, June 3, 1985, p. 76.

31. *Time*, April, 8, 1985, p. 23.

32. Ibid., p. 23.

33. *Newsweek*, August 2, 1993, p. 48.

34. Beasley, *The Betrayal of Health*, p. 161.

35. Ibid.

36. *Newsweek*, August 2, 1993, p. 48.

37. Beasley, *The Betrayal of Health*, p. 149.

38. Ibid., p. 70.

39. Ibid., p. 156.

40. Robert Bellah et al., "Community, Commitment, and Individuality," reprinted in *English* (New York: McGraw Hill, 1993), p. 24.

41. Ibid., p. 30.

42. David Morris, "Deconstructing Community," in *Utne Reader*, March/April 1993, p. 143.

43. Quoted in Carlos Fuentes, "Land of Jekyll and Hyde," *The Nation*, Vol. 242 (March 22, 1986). Reprinted in Mark West, ed., *The Asheville Reader* (Acton, Mass: Copley Publishing, 1992), p. 39.

44. American Council on Education, *What We Don't Know Can Hurt Us* (Washington, D.C.: Division of International Education, 1983), p. 12.

45. Ibid., p. 6.

46. Boorstin, *The Image*, p. 76.

47. Ibid., pp. 74 - 76.

48. Ibid., p. 74.

49. See *Time*, October 8, 1990, pp. 42 - 45; *Time*, June 18, 1990, pp. 30 - 33; *Time*, May 28, 1990, pp. 20 - 22.

Chapter 3

The Heartbreak

I was born into a large polygamous family. At the time of my birth, my father had three wives, including my mother, and about ten children. I grew up in a large house with my mother, grandparents, sisters, brothers, aunts, uncles, cousins, and nieces, all living under the same roof. In my house, we did not have electricity, running water, or any of the modern appliances or conveniences of life. The rooms were few, small and overcrowded. Some people would sleep on the floor without a mattress, except for old clothes converted into blankets.

My childhood environment is rather typical of many Ghanaian traditional households where the extended family arrangement is the rule rather than the exception. In Ghana, and in many parts of Africa, we have an extended family system that consists of many nuclear families affiliated through an extension of the parent-child relationship rather than the husband-wife relationship. In an extended family system, a family is not just husband, wife, and children; it is, rather, a number of households, perhaps hundreds or thousands of people.

Growing up in an African family is fun, interesting, and very challenging. Fun, in the sense of the availability of many playmates and companionship; one seldom gets bored in such a large family setting. Interesting, in the sense that the sheer size of the family opens up a lot of exciting opportunities and possibilities for the pursuit of different interests and goals. Challenging, in the sense that in the shuffle a child can easily get lost, forgotten, and unappreciated. For a child to be fully recognized in such an environment, he must on his own learn to develop his own identity and learn to stay competitive with one's own cousins, age group, brothers and half brothers, and sisters and half sisters.

Discipline is very harsh and crude in the African family when compared with the Western standard. Child discipline can be administered virtually by any one older than the child -- mother, father, uncle, sister, brother, grandparents and family friends. Any of these people who detect any insubordination or lack of obedience or respect on the part of the child can discipline the child without any prior consultation with the parents.

In African societies, it is not uncommon for a child to come home crying because he has been disciplined by his neighbor for some sort of misbehavior. This act is accepted in good faith as something expected of a good neighbor. Africans are not preoccupied with child abuse, and until recently this concept was virtually alien to the African culture. Respect for and obedience to the elderly, be it your older brother or an unrelated older person, are emphasized, and children are expected to acquire these traits at all cost. To enforce this norm, obviously, society accepts strict discipline, which may appear excessive by Western standards.

In my view, this overemphasis on respect and obedience sometimes deprives a child of most of the freedoms needed to develop properly. For example, in many African societies, it is generally regarded as disrespectful for a child to join in a conversation between the elderly, even if he is knowledgeable about the topic, or if he is just interested in learning something about the topic of discussion. A child cannot stand up against an elderly person for his or her rights, no matter what. Children are always wrong when some elderly person disagrees with them. In most traditional African societies, what may be called freedom of speech or discussion is considerably curtailed.

It needs to be emphasized, however, that what may appear to be suppression of individualism or personal freedom in the African family may not necessarily discourage personal initiative and self-reliance. In fact, what it does signify is that the interest of the family is placed above that of the individual. In such a large family, it is rationalized that, if everyone were free to go their own way and do their own thing, there would be nothing but chaos. Control over children's activities and emphasis on respect and obedience are the African means to maintain a closely knit, stable, secure, happy, and trouble-free family and society.

By Western standards, the average African child may not have all the expression of love and affection, but he does not lack attention. The sheer size of the average household is such that the child at any point in time will have some grandparent, aunt, cousin, or brothers and sisters taking care of her. For this reason, most African children feel quite secure, and, until recently, had few of the emotional problems that are prevalent in Western society, and even when they did, they were seldom displayed.

The African child is very much loved. The love, however, is not expressed in the same way that Americans express their love for a child. For an African, love is a very private affair, needing no constant display in public. The African feels secure in his love and commitment and has no urge to demonstrate it every minute. It is very genuine, sincere, and unemotional. It is long lasting and permanent. It is not imagined, or fantasized, but felt, practiced, and not idealized.

So is marriage in African societies. Africans marry into families, not to individuals, and generally try to stay married. Marriage in the "Akan" (my language) means "aware," an extension. To the African therefore, marriage means that you are now extending your (already) extended family to include another extended family.

Once married, your family is thus made up of two extended families. The close ties that develop between these two families during courtship and the nature of the marriage rites performed during the marriage ceremony make it really difficult, and sometimes impossible, to attempt a divorce. The African perception of marriage also makes divorce very difficult to obtain. Africans marry to stabilize and enrich life. For the African, marriage is not an act of emotional impulse or some kind of fantasy. It is a long-deliberated and thought-out process that involves more that the two prospective couples. It is an agreement between families, villages, and clans. A lot is at stake in the marriage that cannot be taken for granted.

An aspect of the African family system that has been a continued source of intrigue to the American and the West in general is polygamy. Polygamy, when practiced, allows a man to marry more than one wife. It is an accepted behavior in African societies. In a polygamous family, the father usually lives with his first wife and the other wives live separately in different homes with their children. But in many instances all the wives may choose to live under the same roof or in the same compound with their husband. In my own case, since my mother was the third wife of my father, I lived with my mother in a different house, while my father lived with his first wife and her children.

Coming from a polygamous family, I would be less than candid if I did say that in today's Africa polygamy is more of a problem than a blessing for the African family. Having more than one wife poses not only economic problems for all the family members, but also other social and family problems. Since invariably more children are to be had in a polygamous family, it is economically difficult to provide all the children with the necessary backgrounds and things they need to do well in a competitive society where opportunities are very few. In addition to economic pressures, the family, and especially the children, have to put up with the seemingly never-ending jealousies and fighting that goes on between the wives, which in time can become infectious and can permanently mar the relationships between half brothers, sisters, and step-mothers. In fact, if it were not for the additional security and support that the extended family gives to children in polygamous family relationships, emotional stress and problems, including suicides, would have been in epidemic proportions in those African societies that practice polygamy.

In Africa, the elderly occupy a place of respect and reverence. Wisdom is generally associated with age, and this is assumed for any elderly person until proven otherwise. The extended family arrangement to a large degree ensures that the elderly live with their children until they pass away. Therefore, to my knowledge, there are no nursing homes or old people's apartments in Africa.

Coming from such a family background, it is not at all surprising that one of my greatest fascinations with America was the American family. I had actually fallen in love with the American family before I arrived in the United States. My image of the American family was one of nuclear, closely knit, and loving groups. The nuclear family typically consists of a married man and woman with their offspring. In the movies that I had watched in Ghana, the American family had been portrayed as stable, cooperative, understanding, close, and unusually kind and considerate.

My first contact with the American family came during my one week of orientation in Accra, Ghana. Brief as my visit was, the image I had of the

American family as well as my expectations were very well met. I stayed with the Pancost family during this week.

The Pancosts may well be classified in the United States as a middle income family, but in Ghana they can easily pass for millionaires. Mr. Pancost, as a diplomat, the director of the United States Information Agency in Ghana, was a very prominent person, and so the family lived extremely comfortably. They had a very large house in one of the exclusive areas in the capital, the airport residential area. They had three cars, three servants, and all the modern appliances they needed to live comfortably. Their living quarters included a large, beautiful garden and an assortment of recreational facilities.

During the week I stayed with them, two of their children were in the house. The younger one, Carol, about thirteen years of age, lived with them in Ghana and attended an American school. The elder one, Keri, about twenty years old, was attending college in one of the midwestern states in the United States. She had come to Ghana that summer, as she did every summer, to spend some time with her family.

Mrs. Pancost had picked me up earlier in the day after my first orientation meeting at the American Embassy. She was driving a large American car with a diplomatic license plate. When we arrived at their huge, beautiful, air-conditioned home, the rest of the family members were out. I was told they would be back in time for a family dinner around 7 p.m.

Meanwhile, I was taken upstairs and shown my room and later offered a snack, together with the good all-American coke. The servants who brought the snack were extremely polite and kind, and they got even better when they knew that I was on my way to the United States. Everybody in Ghana tends to be nice to you once they know you are going to America. They all have heard that America is the land of opportunity and anybody who goes there invariably becomes successful. Being good to you may mean that some day you may pay back the favor one way or the other. Therefore, classmates, friends, and relatives all tend to be nice to you once they are aware you are about to leave for the United States.

After the snack, I retired to my bedroom and took a nap. I was seventeen years old, and it just occurred to me that I had never had a bedroom that I could call my own, however temporary. I could not help reflecting on my own life and telling myself "whatever happens in America, I sure will never be the same." To me, the worst was over. Now my fate rested in my own hands, and I was determined to make the best of it. I could not help repeating one of my favorite lines, "Destiny is not a matter of chance, it is a matter of choice," and I was determined to control mine. Since the initial letter notifying me of my selection for the exchange program, I had observed a consistent transformation in my own life. I felt that some part of my life was giving way for the entry of a new one. At times, I felt that part of my old self was already gone and had been replaced with a new half. This feeling was abruptly brought home to me during my one-week stay with the Pancosts. A new world seemed to have unfolded before my very eyes during the week, and I felt upward bound.

At about 6 p.m., the family seemed to be drifting home one by one. First came in the youngest daughter who was introduced to me as Carol. She was a little shy and didn't talk much. Moments after came her elder sister, who was introduced as Keri. She was friendlier and eager to tell me about what to expect in America. The last to arrive was Mr. Pancost, a very handsome and dignified person. He had a diplomatic air about him and an unmistakable air of importance. Like all the Pancosts, as I found out quickly, he was very kind, interesting, and generous.

Having being introduced to all the family members, and by nature being quite outgoing and not in the least shy, I did not hesitate to seek to impress them about how much I knew about their country, when we finally sat down for dinner at about 7 p.m. We had a very extensive discussion that touched on many aspects of American life; politics, education, dating, church, family, race relations, and many more.

The food was good and had variety. There was the main dish, some kind of casserole, some tossed green salad, some soup, rolls, and dessert. I was overwhelmed not only by the food but also by the way everything had proceeded in the last few hours that I had been with the Pancost family.

Only a few hours before, I did not even know there existed a family called the Pancosts. However, the very few hours I had spent with this family could easily be recorded as some of the happiest in my entire life. I could not remember any time in my life that I had spent more than thirty minutes with my own father discussing things I considered of significance to me. Even when I came home from boarding school, he would spend only minutes inquiring about how much school fee he would have to pay in the coming term. And here I was, pouring my heart out to total strangers, who not only showed interest in my dreams, but were also proud and impressed with the level of my knowledge and maturity. They were sincere and interested in me as a person, willing to do all they could to make my experience in the United States memorable and enjoyable. I was completely overpowered by the love and affection that was expressed to me that evening.

I was equally struck by the freedom, equality, and openness that characterized the discussion and all the activities that took place that evening. Naturally, in my own home, I never sat at the table with my dad or mom to eat together. I ate with my brothers and cousins, usually from the same pot. The meat was usually very scanty and was distributed to each according to his age, with the amount received increasing proportionally with the age.

At dinner, each of the Pancosts in turn related the highlights of their day. The conversation came to an end when Keri's date arrived to pick her up for a movie. Keri had unofficially become my host. However, not being sure when I would be arriving at their home, she had made a previous engagement to see a movie with her boyfriend, an American she had been seeing for some time. She apologized for having to leave me and offered to take me along if I wanted to join them. I thanked her and declined. I did not think it was proper to intrude in her private affairs, at least not on my first day in the family.

My week with the Pancosts was full of joy and good memories. But above all, it confirmed my respect for the American family. Therefore, when I left Ghana for the United States, my feelings toward the American family were nothing less than reverential.

When I arrived at the Portland International Airport, the Robertsons -- Jack, my host father, LaVae, my host mother, Jackie, my host sister, and Lonn, my host brother -- were all there, holding a big sign with my name imprinted on it. They were there as a family, to welcome a new family member. I felt the same way. I considered myself a member of this family and was determined to be one. I did not have to try hard at all. There was an instant flow of affection from both ends, and we all felt like we had known each other for a long time. The letters and pictures we had exchanged had brought us closer than any of us could have imagined.

The Robertsons are a great family -- stable, loving, understanding, cooperative, and, above all, very respectful of each other's rights. My host father, Jack Robertson, runs his own business, Robertson Taxidermy. He is an extremely hard-working and yet a very family-oriented father. He was loving, interesting, kind, understanding, friendly, and above all, fatherly to me, and naturally I felt very close to him. We played tennis and ping pong, and we arm wrestled. I shared my dreams, anxieties, fears, and hopes with him. I also teased him a lot. The year spent with him, and the subsequent holidays I spent with the Robertson family while in college, filled some of the emptiness that I had experienced growing up in an African family.

My host mother, LaVae, is an extraordinary human being. She is understanding, kind, loving, considerate, helpful and very humane. As a mother, she knew when things were not going well and exactly what to do or say. She knew when exactly to leave me alone, particularly on those days that I became homesick and moody, and there were many such days!

My host sister, Jackie, like her mother, was very kind and considerate. She was a junior at Oregon State University when I arrived. She spent very little time at home, coming home only during short breaks and some weekends. Nevertheless, we developed a good family relationship and spent some good times together.

I spent a lot of time with my host brother, Lonn. We were both seniors in the same high school, South Albany High, and we took some classes together. We rode the bus in the mornings together, double-dated sometimes, and had some memorable times together.

It was frequently mentioned to me that the Robertsons were a very unique family. I wouldn't realize the full meaning of this however, until many years later. At that time, I said to myself, the Pancosts had been nice and rather unique too, the Adams (my black American host family in Portland, Oregon) had been equally nice and unique, and indeed, it appeared to me that all the

American families that I had come in contact with, for however brief a time, could easily be classified as nice and rather unique.

During my year as an exchange student, I traveled extensively and met many different American families. I had spent many weekends in various communities, with different families, giving speeches to high schools, churches, and Chambers of Commerce, and not once did I meet a family that I did not like or a family that did not like me either.

Evidently, I met only good, solid, stable American families -- families that have done nothing more than to confirm my positive impressions of the American nuclear family, and thus deepened my fascination and preference for the American family arrangement. As I was to find out later, the American Field Service (AFS) office had deliberately planned the exchange program so that all exchange students would live with the best possible American families in each community. The selection process for "host families" was rather rigorous, requiring not only that all family members be present at the interview, but also that each family member answer specific questions designed to ascertain the stability, strength, love, understanding, and togetherness of the entire family. Obviously, the program aimed at selecting the most ideal, solid, and stable American families to be the host families.

My experiences and encounters with the American family were not to be limited to Oregon. At the end of my year as an exchange student, the AFS organized a national tour for all the participants in the program that year. This tour took us from Portland, Oregon, to New York City. During the three-week national tour, I stayed with many families but found nothing to change my mind about the American family.

To my disappointment and personal horror, this unqualified love affair with the American family was not to last for long. In the winter of 1974, I enrolled as a freshman at Oregon State University and started to date college students and make friends with some of my school and classmates. I also started to watch the American news more regularly, read the newspapers more carefully, and pay attention to what was going on around me.

When I stepped outside my world of the white middle-class enclave and went into the ghettos, met the poor and the lower class American families, I quickly saw some major cracks in the American family. What I found about the American family completely devastated and robbed me of my innocence and destroyed my romance with the American family. I felt mad, misled, and yet very naive. The American family that I had held up on a pedestal was falling apart in my face, and I felt helpless and betrayed.

Only a year ago, I had written letters home to everybody extolling the virtues of the American family and complaining bitterly about how the African child is deprived of love, affection, and adequate attention. In my speeches to various churches, communities, and Chambers of Commerce, I had been critical and unabashedly against polygamy as a family institution.

I had also spoken about the repression of freedom of speech and independence for the African child. I had argued that these were partly responsible for the inability of the Africans, even when they grew up, to speak against political oppression and dictatorship. My argument was that, unless the African child was brought up in freedom, he could not demand freedom once he grew up. I had argued with great conviction that democracy is not only a polity, but it is something much more than that. I had stated that, a people born and raised in a democracy unconsciously acquire ideas and a mental process that make them different from the subjects of a monarchy or dictatorship. We cannot expect African children to be raised in authoritarian families, I maintained, and suddenly grow up to be democrats.

I had also attempted to draw a link between the lack of independence, individualism, and freedom, and the apparent lack of enterprise and innovativeness among African kids who eventually become African leaders. Thus I argued that there should be a greater degree of freedom and independence for the African child. This, I believed, was necessary to induce curiosity and an adventurous and an exploratory spirit in the African child.

But there I was, for the first time presented with a very dark side of the American family, and needless to say, I didn't like what I saw. For example, I did not realize that for many American households, the love, caring, and understanding that seemed to have been so overgenerously supplied to the Pancosts, Robertsons, and Adams were the exceptions rather the rule. Neither did I know that most Americans lacked control over their impulses, with the result being that aggression in the American home had been on the increase for a very long time. In my sheltered life, I did not realize that "battered child" cases had been increasing at an alarming rate and that over 4 million cases were being reported annually, over twenty five thousand of which resulted in permanent brain damage, and about four thousand in death.

Little did I know that the free spirit of the American family when pushed to its ultimate can result in too much sexual freedom and permissiveness to a degree that results in quick and easy divorce. Thus, there is one divorce for every 1.8 marriages, over a million children a year are involved in divorce cases, and nearly 20 million children under eighteen have one or both parents living away from them.

I could not in my wildest imagination expect that over 250,000 illegitimate births take place in the United States and that more than 21 percent of all births occur in the twelve to nineteen age group, with half of these girls unmarried.

I could not believe that the love and affection that were so brilliantly and openly displayed every second toward spouses could so easily be turned off and displayed in a similar fashion and intensity in extramarital affairs, such that half of all divorces in the United States take place because of adultery.

Little did I know that the tremendous amount of freedom that American kids enjoy can so easily be abused and be transformed into freedom to take drugs and to commit crimes. One-third of all American teenagers have experimented with one drug or another, alcoholism and drunkenness are major problems in many schools, and the second leading cause of death among teenagers in this country is suicide.

No, I did not know that each month, 282,000 students (in high schools) are reported as being "disorderly" and that a 1,000 teachers are assaulted seriously enough on school premises to require medical attention and that an additional 125,000 are threatened with bodily harm.

Many Americans who see the homosexual life-style as incompatible with the American traditional family values are predicting that the over fifty cities, towns, and counties, including Detroit, Washington, D.C., and Minneapolis, that have enacted ordinances forbidding discrimination against homosexuals in job and in housing will not only legitimize, but also make it more fashionable and acceptable for children to become homosexuals. This social issue has generated and continues to generate tremendous controversy in the United States. Those who oppose the homosexual life-style see it as an attempt to further undermine the traditional family.

Whatever the merit of the argument above, no one needs to be told that the American family is in trouble when people can march and demonstrate in protest in Chicago because a book entitled *How to Have Sex with Children* had been confiscated by the police. Obviously, the protesters' argument is that freedom of expression in a democracy must guarantee the production and sale of pornographic material and literature, even if it could adversely affect children. I disagree. I believe that democracy without a solid moral and ethical foundation will only lead to social decay, a condition that is abundantly in evidence in the United States today.

Naturally, these are sobering revelations that are as painful as they are true about the dark side of the American family, the building block of the country's civilization. I do not cite these grim statistics about the American family as a way either to embarrass the United States or to condemn the American family. Neither is it my intention to accentuate the positive aspects of the American family. The problems of the American family are highlighted here as a warning to African countries and to Africans who have become as fascinated as I was with the United States, and who believe that everything American is good and must be copied.

In my own country, Ghana, and other African countries, a violent clash of culture is taking place in which the African culture has been pitted against Western culture. The obvious loser is Africa. The perception as it was during the colonial period, and to some extent even today, is that successful Africans are those who have assimilated the Western ways of life and cultural patterns. Thus, Africans are abandoning everything African and in its place are installing Western cultures, values, life-styles, tastes, and preferences. Western music is played in virtually all African nightclubs in preference to African music. African homes are decorated with Western art, and African art and craft are basically produced for the West. When African leaders needed paintings and sculptures to decorate the interior of the Organization of African Unity (OAU) headquarters in Addis Ababa, they recruited Western artists, who turned around and subcontracted Africans artists and sculptors to do the job. Why would African leaders want Western art to decorate one of their historical buildings? This is an insult to the African artist and is unforgivable.

The undermining of African culture by Western culture has been greatly facilitated by Africa's own lack of confidence in its ability and in its people, and by the continent's deep sense of uncertainty about its identity and future. But above all, it has greatly been facilitated by the information technology that has created a global village, where information, news, and events are communicated throughout the world instantaneously.

Today Ghanaians watch the same Cable Network News (CNN) that Americans watch. On Saturdays, the same fashion show seen in the United States, featuring Western concepts of beauty, Western clothes, Western life-styles, and Western behaviors, is presented unadulterated to the Ghanaian public. American movies and books that glorify violence, drugs, sex abuse, and other socially deviant behaviors as the wave of the future are equally available, and Ghanaians are unconsciously buying into them. The effects of all these are already beginning to show. Ghanaians and the rest of the Africans are starting to talk like Americans, dress like Americans, walk like Americans, act like Americans, and finally, soon Ghana and the rest of Africa will be plagued by the same problems that plague the American society today. Africans are copying Americans and doing so very blindly.

The painful truth is that the African family is going through a very difficult time on its own and does not need to import any new problems from the West. What Africa needs is "dealienation." In other words, "reversing the damage that slave trade, colonization, and foreign domination have inflicted on Africa's cultural and spiritual values, on the African identity, and on the African soul."[1] Today, for example, it is unrealistic to talk about the African family any more without making an important distinction between the traditional and the modern African family. Obviously, the traditional family has kept the African family traditions of old. Basically, the emphasis here is on the extended family. In this family, respect is still accorded to the old, obedience and respect for parental authority are stressed, and kinship bonds and loyalty to the family are stressed. In this family unit, group rather than individual interest is considered supreme. The polygamous marriage arrangement has meant that African women have been and continue to be at the forefront of the battle for economic self-reliance for Africa. Today, more than 60 percent of the food produced in Africa is produced by women. However, this production has not meant any significant economic freedom for women. This is mainly because, even though women may be the producers of agricultural output, Africa, like the rest of the world, is still a male-dominated society, and the inheritance and succession laws in Africa were not developed with the interest of women in mind. For example, the Akans of West Africa have a matrilinear type of inheritance, an arrangement whereby a man is succeeded by his nephews and not by his children. In most such cases, the woman who may have been the economic mainstay of the family may lose her inheritance from her husband to the husband's family and must invariably struggle to support the children from such marriages.

In addition, whereas before children were viewed largely as economic assets in terms of their contributions as farm labor, today, this is not the case. Having more children means having to pay more school fees, and to pay more for good and nutritional diets, clothes, and medical expenses. This has become a drain on the meager family resources, thus putting additional pressure on African women to work increasingly more and harder to support the family. I know this from personal experience.

At the time I was growing up my father had three wives. When the time came for me to go to boarding school, with so many children to take care of, my father decided that he would pay the boarding school fees for one of each of his wives' children. Since my elder brother was already in boarding school I had no chance of ever getting to a boarding school. So my mother sent me to boarding school and supported me with the help of scholarships throughout my secondary school education. Had it not been for her determination, hard work, and foresight, I would not be writing this book today.

Naturally, in view of my African background, my disappointment with the American family is not limited to the nuclear family alone, but it extends to the way America treats its elderly. The American treatment of the elderly is exactly the opposite of what happens to the elderly in Africa. In Africa, an elderly person is expected to act his age, not to conceal it. The elderly generally occupy a place of respect and reverence, and this is an enduring African virtue. Pretending to be young or trying to appear young when you are not is considered vain in Africa and is frowned upon. In the traditional African family, wisdom and respect are associated with age.

The elderly in Africa most often live with their children who are expected to take care of their parents in their old age as their parents took care of them in their infancy. Thus, there are no nursing homes, and the elderly are not viewed as people who have outlived their productive lives and so can be disposed of.

An episode at Marshal Field's in Chicago demonstrates the Americans obsession to appear youthful. On this day hundreds of disappointed customers placed their order at $195 each for an out-of-stock introductory kit of glycol, a new line of skin care products. Similarly, in New York City, a few lucky people managed to part with $300 for assorted glycol lotions and potions. An increasing number of Americans are spending millions of dollars to stay and appear young.

In 1985, Americans paid a hefty $1.2 billion to stay and appear young. In America it is not a complement to tell someone that he or she is old. Americans want to stay young forever, and they do all they can to achieve that desire.

American optimism sometimes appears to even defy reason. And the American instinctive "can-do" attitude propels them to challenge something as certain as old age to resist fiercely and to fight against it with all available means -- with plastic surgery, dieting, exercising, and cosmetics. I do not blame Americans for doing this. Certainly, they do this for a very good reason, knowing their own attitudes toward old people and the way they treat their elderly people. They want to avoid being accorded the same treatment, so Americans desperately seek every available means to stay young. There are about 36 million elderly people in this country, and they are referred to as senior citizens. This title "senior citizen" is quite impressive, for it suggest that perhaps they may be entitled to some privileged position in society. But this is not so. The United States is a capitalist throw away society. In such capitalist societies where personal relationships and loyalty are not allowed to stand in the way of profits, many senior citizens, having exhausted their most productive years, are now as disposable as a piece of garbage. They are the rejects of society; they have outlived their usefulness!

A substantial number of elderly Americans live alone on fixed incomes and in drab apartments. They struggle for the bare necessities of life and are largely ignored by their children. Many of them are sick most of the time and are lonely and scared of crime and apprehensive about their bleak future. Most Americans know that this is the kind of fate that awaits them when they grow old. If this is indeed what happens to people in the United States when they grow old is it surprising that nobody wants to grow old?

In spite of many virtues and the positive attributes of the traditional African family, the African traditional family system, like the American family, is under siege. One of the most obvious shifts currently taking place in the African family is the changing roles of males and females, with females becoming increasingly more independent and assertive of their rights. Africa is not indifferent to the irresistable currents of women's liberation that are sweeping the world. But for all practical purposes, the African women's struggle for "liberation" may be different from the kind of liberation that American women are fighting for.

Most African countries do not have any institutionalized or legalized sets of rules aimed at discrimination against women. In practically all cases, women who do the same work as men are paid equally. However, there are many acts of discrimination against women that are based on what can generally be considered "culturally based discrimination." Some of this discrimination tends to exclude women from certain ownership rights, so that women cannot own land outright, other cultural practices create the woman's excessive dependence on men for their economic needs. For example, in Zaire, women are required to get the approval of their husbands to be able to participate in certain economic activities. This type of cultural discrimination tends to affect rural and illiterate women (majority of women) more than educated urban women.

In many African countries, the educated elite, both males and females, generally tend to have little professional contact, and especially commonality of interests, with the rural poor. The feminist movement in Africa is generally led by the urban elite. For these reasons, the feminist agenda, to the extent that it deals with equality, has had a very narrow focus, being aimed largely at seeking equality between elite African women and elite African men.

But much as has happened in the United States, African women who have achieved equality with men, in work outside the home have become subjected to the same pressures, anxiety, and the frustrations that have bedeviled their husbands and men in general. These women have increasingly manifested some, even if substantially less, of the same problems that the American family has recently become known for: high divorce rates, stress, infidelity, and other forms of alienation. The general economic decline in Africa which has, on one hand, increased African women's responsibilities has, on the other hand, economically marginalized the African woman. Today, African women have to serve not only as cooks, but also as nurses, cleaners, breadwinners, and heads of households.

The African child, the center of the African family, is also going through a very difficult and painful transition, a process similar to the one their parents are going through. As a result of Western educational influences, television, movies, books, and travels abroad, African children are becoming more independent, more assertive of their rights, more aggressive, and more individualistic. These behaviors are incompatible with the ideals and values of the traditional African family.

It is increasingly being claimed that African children today are being alienated from African culture. However incompatible, these changes are being embraced as the inevitability of change, although it is hoped that the true and full effect on the African family will not be too devastating. However, the handwriting is already on the wall. Increasingly, Africa is being beset by drug abuse, teenage pregnancies, high dropout rates from schools, and other forms of alienation unknown before in Africa, such as homosexuality.

This discussion of the American and African families shows that both families need to be liberated. For the American family, liberation consists not only in the intellectual sense, but in mind, body, and the emotions. The United States needs a dialectical liberation from the contradictions and alienation that have developed and enveloped its entire society. I am acutely aware that effecting this liberation is far easier said than done. How can a powerful nation be asked to liberate from its well functioning, rich, powerful, and civilized state that is the dream and envy of many countries? But so it must to reinvent itself, as it has done so many times when it has faced crises.

For the African family, the need has never been greater to achieve liberation from too much inhibition and negative traditional and cultural demands. While the problem with the United States appears to be one of extreme permissiveness and individualism, in Africa the problem is clearly inadequate expression and manifestations of love and affection and insufficient freedom and individualism. Africa must find an appropriate balance that will allow it to temper American values, life-styles, and materialism with its own humanity, spirituality, and sense of community. Africa's humanity and spirituality cannot be sacrificed for

American materialism, permissiveness, and individualism.

For both the United States and Africa, the challenge lies in finding the appropriate balance that will ensure family stability and the nurturing of children. Thus, Africans and Americans alike must acknowledge the family as the key to national stability and the importance of the family rather than the individual as the basic unit of society and the core of political and economic life. Even more importantly, it is imperative for both societies to realize that an essential need for the survival of the family is protection from violence and aggression, either from external sources or even from self-induced wounds. Ramatoulaye, an African woman activist, said it best: "The nation is made up of all the families, rich or poor, united or separated, aware or unaware. The success of a nation therefore depends inevitably on the family."[2]

NOTES

1. Haskeu G. Ward, *African Development Reconsidered* (New York: A Phelps-Stokes Institute Publication, 1989), p. 119.

2. Mariama Ba, *So Long A Letter* (Portsmouth, New Hampshire: Heinemann Educational Books Inc., 1981), p. 89.

Chapter 4

Voter Apathy and Media Politics

"Government of the people,
by the people and for the
people."
Abraham Lincoln

The dismantling of the Berlin Wall and the fall of the Iron Curtain, as well as the emancipation of Eastern and Central Europe from totalitarian regimes, signaled to the world, especially the developing world, the inevitability of change and a strong and irresistible force for democracy. Some have even ventured to say that these events have created a new world order, and that an important component of this order is a renewed emphasis on respect for fundamental human rights, democracy, and freedom.

The call for democracy and freedom echoes across the globe. Donor nations, especially the United States, Britain, Japan, Germany, and France, and international development organizations, such as the World Bank and the International Monetary Fund (IMF) have tied their economic aid to countries that undertake political reforms guaranteeing political pluralism, democracy, freedom, and respect for human rights.[1] This condition on aid is referred to as "aid with democratization strings."

The effect of all this is that Africa is going through an unprecedented era of political reforms supposedly aimed at democratizing its authoritarian political systems. Several African countries including Gabon, Congo, Angola, Ghana, Nigeria, Togo, Kenya, Ivory Coast, and Zambia have joined the democratization bandwagon in order to either retain or increase their Western aid.

The so-called democratization process has not meant the institutionalization of democracy in Africa. To the contrary, Africans are increasingly finding that while the idea of democracy is durable, its practice is precarious. My own country, Ghana, has just gone through a charade of an exercise that was meant to restore true democracy to the country after over a decade of bloodthirsty dictatorship under Jerry Rawlings and his Provisional National Defense Council (PNDC).

In Ghana and elsewhere in Africa -- Burkina Faso, Ivory Coast, Kenya, Cameroon, and Nigeria -- the reform process has not produced the desired democratic outcome. What we actually have in all of these countries is "democratization without democracy." The so-called democratization process has become a ritual whose outcome is predetermined to legitimize either a corrupt, illegitimate, or autocratic regime in Africa.

In Ghana, the so-called democratization process provided a convenient pretext for the transformation of Jerry Rawlings' military dictatorship into a constitutional dictatorship. This has caused a great deal of skepticism in Africa about the credibility of the process; thus, many Africans are apprehensive about the current democratization drive and about the prospects for true democracy in Africa any time soon.

There is increasingly little faith in using the ballot box as a means of changing governments in Africa. Therefore, African governments continue to be changed not peacefully through the ballot box, but through military coups d'etat. And in most cases, once power has been usurped, it is seldom surrendered voluntarily. African presidents became presidents for life. To get rid of them, you either have to kill them or overthrow them. As a result, coups have become in Africa what elections are to the West. More than fifteen countries in Africa have had one coup since they gained independence, and more than thirteen have had two or more. By 1982, no fewer than forty-eight of the fifty-three governments in Africa had been overthrown, and in more than twenty African countries there have been attempted, but unsuccessful, coups d'etat. As Shegu Shagari, former president of Nigeria, painfully admitted after having been overthrown by the military in Africa, "At the end of the day, there are only two political parties in Nigeria -- the military and the civilians."

Even though coups have generally installed governments unable to successfully deal with Africa's economic, political, and social problems, they continue to occur. Tribalism, poor economic conditions, political corruption, and ineffective political systems are contributing causes. But most important is Africa's inability to develop and sustain a political culture that supports democratic principles such as tolerance, compromise, dialogue, and free speech, all of which are requisites for successful electoral systems. Without strong and institutionalized electoral systems, the unbridled personal ambitions of a politicized and radicalized African military personnel compel military intervention in politics, despite its devastating effect on the political, social, and economic development of the continent.

In their attempts to tighten their grips on power, and otherwise effectively control their subjects, African governments have tended to close the valve of public expression and dissent. Those who disagree with governments are branded as dissidents.

Invariably, those with the ability and or the intelligence to either challenge, or to offer a different perspective to an African government, are either killed, jailed or exiled. This deprives African citizens of a fundamental democratic prerequisite-- an intelligent and articulate opposition.

African governments also seek to control the thought process of their people. Not surprisingly, the government controls radio, newspapers, and television and analyzes every utterance to determine where a person's loyalty lies. The news media reports what the governments want reported, and many times what you hear and what you see are irreconcilable.

In Africa it seems that Big Brother is watching every move made by the people. In time, most principled and decent people leave the government.

Gradually, African leaders are surrounded only by gaping sycophants, ready to cheat, kill, and sometimes even die for their masters. Given the Africans' incredible ability to tolerate the brutality, abuse, and idiosyncracies of their leaders, dictatorships in Africa tend to last far too long, usually until another coup takes place.

The cycle of violence and social and economic disruption and dislocation continues unabated. This has largely been the lot of most of Africa's post independent history. There are no redeeming values. It is a sad state of affairs. The Africans' optimistic expectations and the euphoria over their freedom and economic prosperity at the dawn of independence in the early 1960s, have largely given way to a political nightmare of abuse, dictatorship, civil war, tribalism, and a political tradition of intolerance and life presidencies.

Today, Africa has begun a new search for democratic institutions that will blend its native political institutions and cultural traditions with those necessary for democratic government. But Africans cannot, and must not, remain immune to the tremendous political and economic reforms that are sweeping the rest of the world.   Africa cannot be secluded from the realities of global interdependence. Thus, the political institutions that Africa selects must be able to respond to the global conditions of the twenty-first century.

The issue is not about the need for democracy in Africa, as much as it is about what kind of democracy and what Africans can do to avoid the problems that currently plague older democracies, such as the United States. Some observers, including both Africans and Westerners, believe that the American brand of democracy will serve Africa quite well. Others, including the author, believes that while Africa can learn a great deal from the American system, it should be careful not to copy the American system blindly. I believe this debate is a healthy and necessary one. If Africa is to adopt the American concept of democracy, then Africans need to examine all aspects of the American system in order to identify its inherent weaknesses.

The American system of government is based on the concept that authority flows from the people to the government. Jefferson was most eloquent about this when he said, "to serve these rights, governments are instituted among men, deriving their just powers from the consent of the governed." Abraham Lincoln expressed the same idea in his famous Gettysburg address, "Government of the people, by the people and for the people."

These statements embody the principles of democracy, which encourage (and revolve around) a popular participation in the political process. One of the major guarantees of a democracy is the conferring of universal suffrage which allows the free exercise of voting in freely and fairly contested elections.

If a government is to be one "of the people, for the people and by the people," then not only should there be voter participation in the election and the political process, but also the voter must be reasonably well informed about policy issues and must have an opinion on these issues. Moreover, for a mandate to be valid, the electorate must be well informed about public issues, and political parties should provide the voters with candidates who represent diverse policy-oriented choices. The ideal model of democracy requires that political parties offer voters policy alternatives that are clearly articulated and that the parties compete for votes on the basis of contrasting programs. This is the essence of the American democracy that the developing world talks about so much and that is being offered as the alternative to the various authoritarian, autocratic regimes throughout the world, especially the developing world.

I believe that the American system of government, and indeed the fundamental institutions of its democratic culture, are under siege in the United States from all fronts. It is been undermined by the pervasive influence of the media, political action committees (PACs), and apathy among the American populace. The ideal of the citizen politician, dramatized in the movie, *Citizen Kane,* has only nostalgic value in American politics today. Politics in the United States, like that in Africa, has become a profession. Once people enter politics, they stay, and they become permanent, full-time professionals. For example, in a third straight election, 96 percent of the incumbents in the United States House of Representatives were reelected in the 1990 midterm election.[2]

In this, and the next chapter, I will examine the many intractable problems that confront America's democracy. I will show that in the United States, apathy and the media, especially television, are undermining the foundations of democracy. This chapter demonstrates that, in spite of the glaring successes of the American political system, there are equally glaring problems that other countries, especially African countries, must avoid.

This chapter is designed to caution Africans that as new political structures are designed and developed, they must strive to avoid problems that currently afflict the U.S. democracy. For example, although the U.S. political system does not suffer from military interventions and disruptions, it occasionally has to deal with politicians who may want to subvert the political system.

When President Richard Nixon wanted to subvert the American democratic system, he was forced to resign. The example illustrates that the United States has developed the necessary political, social, and economic institutions that, in large part, guard against certain human frailties. The system is able to check abuses of power and other dictatorial tendencies such as consuming political ambition, lust for power, and greed, which have generally caused African leaders to become dictators or to declare themselves presidents for life. James Madison, sensitive to the potential abuse of power by politicians, wrote in the *Federalist Paper* 51, the following:

But what is government itself, but the greatest of all reflections on human nature? If men were angels, no government would be necessary. If angels were to govern men, neither external nor internal controls on government would be necessary. In framing a government which is to be administered by men over men, the great difficulty lies in this: you must first enable the government to control the governed; and in the next place oblige it to control itself. A dependence on the people is, no doubt, the primary control on the government; but experience has taught mankind the necessity of auxiliary precautions.[3]

Evidently, Madison was concerned about restraining the popular will and hedging it about with constitutional limits.

The "auxiliary precautions" are the checks and balances system that pits different governing elites against each other. The dependence on the people is incorporated in the electoral institutions. Dependence on the people requires that the electorate have some control over their representatives. This ensures that the representative's interests are identified with those of the community. One of the most effective ways to do this is to regulate their tenure in office through frequent elections. Elections thus provide a linkage between preferences of the electorate and actions of government.

Elections, in effect, legitimize government actions and use of power, on the presumption that elected officials act in the name of the people. Beyond this, elections promote stability in the political system by offering the electorate the opportunity to decide political secession and controversial public policy. One of my major disappointments with the American political system is the low degree of voter participation in the electoral process. I believe that a most important factor in sustaining the credibility of democracy is to ensure a high level of voter participation in the electoral process. Yet voter participation in the United States today is at its lowest in decades; it hovers around only 50 percent. While elections by themselves do not serve as policy mandates or provide assurance that democracy will work, they do function as symbolic reassurances to the masses. Today, nearly half of the adult population in America fails to vote, even in presidential elections. Since the 1960 presidential race, voter turnout has steadily declined, from 64 percent of the eligible voters to 53 percent in the election in 1992. Turnout is even lower in off-year congressional races and local elections.

Election turnout figures in the United States are lower than those of most other democracies. This is especially the case if turnout figures are based on total adult population. The turnout in recent elections has been 74 percent in Japan, 77 percent in Great Britain, 88 percent in West Germany and 93 percent in Italy.

It is important that in a democracy, voters, if not completely informed, must at least be aware of the broad outlines of programs, political events and facts, and policies advocated by candidates, in order to be able to have opinions on them. The classical democracy theory stresses the need for a citizenry that is highly motivated to participate in public affairs and that has substantial interest and concern about such matters. The democratic theory puts the burden on a rational citizen's capability to choose among competing alternatives on the basis of accurate information and sound reasoning. To play their roles fully in a democratic system, citizens must acquire information to help them to decide how to vote and form opinions with which they can influence government policy formulation.

Bernard Berelson and Associates, in their study of voting behavior in the United States, found that, instead of being informed, interested, and rational, "voters were found to be ignorant, apathetic, and irrational"[4]   A large percentage of the American electorate are pathetically uninformed and inarticulate. Public opinion analysts have reported that only about one-half of the American public knew the elementary fact that each state, for instance, has two senators. Fewer still knew the length of the terms of members of Congress or the number of Supreme Court justices.

Aside from their ability to identify the president, most people can identify only one other visible public figure, usually the governor of their state. A 1982 Gallup poll reported that only 46 percent of the voters knew the name of their representative in Congress, while another poll showed that only 62 percent knew their representative's party affiliation. Fewer yet, 21 percent, knew how the representative voted on any major bill.

This lack of public knowledge about political facts, public issues and officials is not limited to adults alone. It is just as bad with American youths. A nationwide survey of seventeen and eighteen year olds found that only 45 percent knew who represented them in Congress; only 65 percent could name the three branches of the federal government; only 32 percent could name the chief justice of the United States; and only 67 percent knew that the Democrats rather than the Republicans controlled the House of Representative. Few of my own students could name the secretaries of state, treasury, defense, or the chairman of the Federal Reserve Board. Less than half could give the full name of the vice president of the United States, and fewer still could name the speaker of the House of Representative.

Despite the controversy and the intense publicity over U.S. public policy in Central America, in 1983 the vast majority of the American public did not know which side the Reagan administration supported in either El Salvador or the conflict in Nicaragua. Only 8 percent of the public knew that the Reagan administration supported the government of El Salvador and the insurgents in Nicaragua.

Is the Americans apathetic attitude to politics a failure of the American democracy or a reflection of its success? Some would argue that the tremendous apathy to politics in the United States is due to its success. This argument holds that many Americans have become complacent and perhaps too confident that the system will inexorably produce a desirable outcome with or without their participation. Thus, they have concluded that they do not need to actively participate in the electoral process for it to work, and so they choose to dance themselves into political oblivion.

It has also been argued that the low voter turnout may be due to the fact the United States does not make it easier for voters to register compared to other nations. In other words, the U.S. registration procedures deter many people from voting.[5]

Many others, however, argue that the low voter participation in the political process serves as an indictment of the American democratic process. Instead of seeking to empower the masses, the process has tended to alienate them. Increasingly, the average American does not feel he can influence the political process, that a few political elites control the system, and no matter what individuals do, there cannot be any meaningful change. Today, 60 percent of the American public agrees that "people like me don't have any say about what the government does."[6] Angus Campbell's American Voter study findings support this. The study concludes that "citizens with higher level of interest in politics, greater concern about the election outcome, and *greater feelings of effectiveness in influencing political affairs* were more apt to vote.[7] (emphasis mine). The fact of the matter is that neither of these arguments employed to explain the cause of voter apathy in the United States bode well for the future of American democracy. As W. Lance Bennett puts it, "The disturbing possibility is that many voters have come to accept, whether angrily, cynically, or apathetically, an electoral system that grows more dysfunctional with each election."[8] The decline of voter participation clearly questions the legitimacy and mandate of government and may perhaps have contributed to the increasing institutional paralysis and leadership vacuum in Washington, D.C. Kevin Phillips believes that Washington has become incapable of leading the nation. "From the White House to Capitol Hill, the critical weakness of American politics and governance is becoming woefully apparent: a frightening inability to define and debate emerging problems. For the moment, the political culture appears to be brain-dead," he declares.[9]

In American voter studies, Campbell et al. concluded that less than a third of the Americans had any opinion on public issues, were aware of what the government was doing, and perceived a difference between the two parties. They concluded that it is probable that two-thirds of the electorate make a choice unrelated to any issue raised by the candidates in their campaign.[10] During the 1980 election, even as far into the election as October, 52 percent of the eligible voters were unaware of Jimmy Carter's stand on inflation and unemployment while 47 percent were unaware of Ronald Regan's stand on the same issues. In addition, a significant proportion of the eligible voters were unaware of the two candidates' stand on such important issues as domestic expenditures, defense spending, and on the U.S.-Russia relationship.[11]

Why is there so much lack of opinion and information on topics of public policy? The same factors that explain low voter participation in elections also explain the absence of opinion and information. According to William Flanigan, "individuals with little interest in or concern with politics are least likely to have opinions on matters of public policy." He continues, "low socio-economic status is associated with no opinion on issues: low income and little education create social circumstances in which individuals are less likely to have views and information on public choices."[12] In effect, the poor masses abdicate their democratic rights to the political elites.

But the masses are not only generally poorly informed; they also demonstrate an acute inability to sort out and relate the information they possess. Frequently, people will support two candidates with fundamentally different positions. They do this generally because they are not properly informed about the positions these candidates represent. Another possible reason for this inconsistency is the influence of public opinion polls. Many times the questions asked in these polls are contradictory and meaningless. But does this suggest that voters are fools? An expert on American elections has characterized the rationale of voter behavior as follows.

Most of them are not interested in most public issues most of the time. In a society like ours, it apparently is quite possible to live comfortably without being politically concerned. Political activity is costly and eats up time and energy at an astounding rate.[13]

Incidentally, this is the same response I received from my students when I asked them why they show so little in interest in politics today. Most of the students said that they were busy trying to work to support themselves and did not have the time to get involved in political issues. Like my students, the voters characterized above do not seem to realize that policies made by politicians eventually determine whether or not they can buy a house, a car, get a job, and how much taxes they will pay.

For many voters, the cost of being politically uninformed far outweighs any savings made from abstaining from politics. For Thomas Jefferson once said, "If a nation expects to be ignorant and free in a state of civilization, it expects what never was and never shall be."[14] This is as true for individual voters as it is for a nation.

Those who think that voters are fools tend to believe that they are not really fools per se, but that they only act like fools. They do so because politicians give them no option. Voters are presented with poor and unarticulated choices and are seldom invited to the public decision-making process.[15] Indeed, voters wish elections were issue-oriented. In 1988, for example, while 63 percent of the voters said that issues were the most important factor in choosing a president, fewer than 10 percent voting in the presidential election felt that the candidates addressed the important ones. [16]

If the electorate is so uninformed, then it may be expected to vote along ideological lines. However, this is not supported by the facts. When social scientists first examined the entire electorate in the United States in the 1950s, they found that ideological commitments were significant in the political decisions of only a tiny fraction of the voters. Three percent of the total electorate were ideologues, 10 percent were near ideologues and the remainder displayed no ideological content in their evaluation of political decisions. [17]

Today, one can classify 33 percent of the electorate as having an ideology or 40 percent with a near ideology. Most ideologues tend to be highly educated and can understand the policy questions and issues in the campaign. These individuals are also more likely to view their jobs and wealth as dependent on political decisions made during elections.

A high point for ideological voting in America was 1964 when Lyndon Johnson ran against Barry Goldwater. Since 1964, ideological voting has steadily and consistently declined. In 1972, when Richard Nixon defeated the liberal George McGovern, voting on the basis of ideology did not increase. In the election of 1976 in which Jimmy Carter opposed Gerald Ford, ideological voting actually decreased. However, the 1980 race between Reagan and Carter brought back some ideological voting, though not as much as had been expected.

If the electorate is not voting according to ideology, perhaps he may be voting according to his political party affiliations. But again my investigations showed otherwise. In the United States, the two major political parties are the Republican and the Democratic parties. Forty-three percent of Americans are registered as Democrats, and 30 percent as Republicans, with 27 percent being Independents. Voting along pure party lines would definitely benefit the Democratic party. But this has not always been the case.

The facts are that only a few Americans (generally black Americans and other small minorities) consistently vote along party lines at the presidential level. If Americans do not in general vote according to ideological beliefs or along party lines, then how do they vote, and what determines the candidate who gets the vote of the average American voter?

The discussions above show clearly that the American voter is not a perfectly informed citizen with fixed policy preferences who votes according to ideology or on partisan lines. Rather, American voters possess only limited and imperfect information about politics. They know only vaguely what the government is doing, what alternative and competing policies can be pursued, and how those policies will affect their interests. It therefore becomes the task of political parties to inform, to educate, and to persuade the voters. This can be done only if political parties offer clear choices and alternatives, and a good articulation of the consequences of various policy outcomes.

The inability or the unwillingness of political parties to offer clear choices for the electorate, combined with increasingly lower voter participation and apathy, has meant that the political elite, principally the rich, the media, and special interest groups, have increased the level of their influence over the American political process and in the process have perverted American politics. Their activities may also be undermining the very foundations of the American democratic political process.[18]

Because national elections are not high in ideological or issue content and are influenced rather insignificantly by party affiliation, candidates base their appeals on the economic condition of the times and on their personal characteristics. And where can these appeals be most effective than television images? American television has become the battleground upon which elections are fought. The effect is that communication in the American political system flows downward from the political candidates to the masses, and television and the news media have become the means by which not only information, but also values, attitudes, and emotions are communicated to the people.

As Murray Edelman, a political scientist, would argue, "For most people most of the time politics is a series of pictures in the mind, placed there by television news newspaper, magazines, and discussions. . . . Politics for most of us is a passing parade of symbols."[19] It appears that in American politics, "the elites instruct the masses about politics and social values and shape public opinion and discussion through television, the most potent and major source of information for majority of Americans." The press has assumed the role of organizing public opinion, but it must be the reverse. As Walter Lippmann said in 1921, "My conclusion is that public opinions must be organized for the Press if they're to be sound, not by the Press as is the case today."[20]

The ascendancy of the age of television has irreversibly shifted the content and meaning of public discourse. For television, discourse is generally conducted through visual imagery, the conversation that television gives us is in imagery rather than in words. Whereas there has been a significant decline in the number of speechwriters, there has been a concomitant increase in the number of image makers in politics. The image makers are changing the way politics is conducted in the United States. American politics today has become showmanship. And politicians have now become actors, while actors have become politicians.

In the process, Americans have developed a new culture, which Neil Postman, who has written extensively on the pervasive role of television in American life in general, believes has caused all public discourse to assume an entertainment format, such that "American politics, religion, news, athletics, education, and commerce have been transformed into congenial adjuncts of show business, largely without protest or even much popular notice."[21] The result is that everything in America is trivialized, to the extent that important and serious public business cannot be discerned from trivial pursuits. Thus, he concludes, today Americans are in danger of amusing themselves to death.

The fictional Boston political boss, Frank Skeffington, emphasizing the political realities in America and the pervasive role of showmanship in American politics when he said, "politics is the greatest spectator sport in America." But Ronald Reagan said it best when in 1966 he declared, "Politics is just like show business."[22] Indeed, having succeeded in Hollywood show business, he left to join political show business, serving two terms as president.

But is politics really like show business, or, better yet, should American politics be like show business? Postman says no and argues that show business is intent on pleasing the crowd, and its "principal instrument is artifice." If politics is like show business, then no virtue will be attached to it. If politics is allowed to become show business, then would politicians not lose their sense of mission and purpose, their sense of public service, martyrdom, their pursuit of excellence, and honesty? Would they not be engaged only in glitz and glitter, in make-believe, and in self-delusion? [23] In show business, the quest is to attain the status of celebrity. In politics, the objective is to render a public service.

By bringing to bear on politics all of the arts of show business -- music, drama, imagery, humor and celebrity -- Postman says, "television has devastated political discourse" in the United States. So in American politics, style has replaced substance, and whether or not a politician wins or loses is determined by how he appears on television, the image he projects on television, the impressions he creates on television, how he fixes his gaze, his smiles, his make-up, and how he delivers his one-liners, and how they are received by the audience.

When it comes to political campaigns in America, the line between what is show business and what is not is increasingly difficult to identify. It should thus not come as a surprise to anyone then that those who control television and the news media also control politics and public opinion.

George Orwell in his book *1984* expressed profound fears about the spiritual devastation created by tyranny in the West. Ironically, Orwell's prophecy has less relevance to the United States today than the prophecy of Aldous Huxley. Orwell wrongly predicted that the control of society's thought would come from some authoritarian government. It would have a Ministry of Truth, tracking individual activities, ready to record people's surreptitious activities. He couldn't have been more wrong.

Huxley, on the other hand, believed that in the age of technology, spiritual devastation was more likely to come from a very familiar or trusting face, even perhaps from a more user-friendly environment. He was talking about the pervasive impact of the electronic media, especially television, on society. In the Huxleyan prophecy, Big Brother does not watch us, by his choice; we watch him, by ours. There is no need for wardens or gates or for a Ministry of Truth. As Postman states, "when a population becomes distracted by trivia, when cultural life is redefined as a perpetual round of entertainments, when serious public conversation becomes a form of baby-talk, when, in short, a people become an audience, and their public business a vaudeville act, then a nation finds itself at risk; cultural death becomes a clear possibility."[24]

Huxley's prophecy is manifested in America today. Television has invaded practically every household in the nation: 98 percent of all American homes have television sets, and more than 90 million Americans watch television every night. But the danger is not that Americans watch television or that television has invaded every home. The danger lies in the fact that American television has not limited itself to providing trivialities. Rather, "it professes to carry important cultural and political messages that have become the basis for important political decisions." In effect, television has successfully elevated irrelevance and trivialities into credible political facts that the public consumes without notice or serious reflection. As Edward Herman and Noam Chomsky conclude:

Leaders of the media claim that their news judgements rest on unbiased, objective criteria. We contend, on the other hand, that the powerful are able to fix the premise of discourse, decide what the general populace will be allowed to see, hear, and think about, and "manage" public opinion by mounting regular propaganda campaigns, aimed at shaping public opinion on important public issues.[25]

Today, over two-thirds of the American public concedes that television provides most of their news on world events and in America. And over two-thirds of the public says that television is its most trusted news source. A few years ago the question of whether American television reflected American culture or shaped it was seriously debated; today the question is largely moot. Television has become the American culture.

The impact of television on American public opinion is significant because it conveys not only information but also emotion. The Reagan campaign advertisements during the 1984 election that showed him standing by the demilitarized zones between the two Koreas, the World War II memorials in West Germany, and at the Berlin Wall, all provoked strong images that were successfully exploited to his advantage. Modern politics has become increasingly remote to the average American voter while reliance on television has increased. Politicians know the emotive power of television and have capitalized on it. But television has not always had as decisive an influence on American politics as it does now.

The politicians' increased involvement in television programs and the amusement industry in general did not start until the late 1950s and did not become general until the 1980s. Writing in 1961, V. O. Key characterized the press as "a common carrier" of the message of America's political elite, "while others likened it to a mirror held up to society."[26] Conducting panel surveys during the elections of 1940 and 1948, Paul Lazarsfeld and Bernard Berlson found that a candidate's media exposure seldom changed people's mind. They concluded that "voters' opinions were molded by their party and social allegiances -- allegiances that undermined the media's ability to change attitudes."[27]

But all this has changed. The media have gained significant influence over the electorate because voters have come to depend heavily on the information they provide. The erosion of voters' partisan loyalties has also contributed greatly to the increased influence of the media on elections in the United States. In contrasts of the parties' hold on the electorate has significantly declined.[28]

Senator Everett Dirksen, who was one of the first politicians to make the foray into the industry, once appeared as a guest on "What's My Line?" John F. Kennedy allowed his house to be invaded by Ed Murrow's "Person to Person." Richard Nixon also appeared for a few seconds on "Laugh-in."

By the 1980s, however, it had become quite obvious that any serious political candidate must learn how to combine television showmanship and political showmanship to get anywhere. Both vice presidential candidate William Miller and Sam Ervin of Watergate fame did a television commercial for American Express. Former president Gerald Ford joined the former secretary of state, Henry Kissinger, for brief roles on "Dynasty." Massachusetts governor Michael

Dukakis, and later the Democratic party nominee for president, appeared on "St. Elsewhere," and the speaker of the House, Tip O'Neil, appeared on "Cheers." [29]

Overnight, it had not only become fashionable but also a necessity for politicians to become entertainers as well as celebrities. Americans had officially accepted the fusion of Hollywood showmanship with political showmanship culminating in the transformation of actor Ronald Reagan into President Ronald Reagan in 1980.

The power to determine what Americans will see and hear about lies with the three major private television networks: the American Broadcasting Company, the Columbia Broadcasting System, and the National Broadcasting Corporation. There are also many local privately owned television stations licensed by an agency of the federal government, the Federal Communication Commission (FCC), to use broadcasting channels. Because of the high cost of producing news and entertainment, these small television stations have chosen to affiliate themselves with the three major networks in order to have access to their news and entertainment programs. It is the top executives of these corporations who occupy the most powerful and privileged positions in America and who the former vice president, Spiro Agnew, referred to as a "tiny, enclosed fraternity of privileged men." The top network executives -- the presidents, vice presidents, directors, and producers -- determine the news, the entertainment and the amount of violence that Americans are allowed to see on their televisions. These individuals and their networks have become king-makers, shakers, and setters of national agendas, policies, and public opinions. As king-makers, television coverage can, and often does create instant celebrities, or shall we call them political candidates?

The thin line between informing the public about a person's achievement often blurs into the promotion of the individual for a run for public office. Thus, television exposure, whether for an interview or a special documentary, can create instant celebrity. A good example of this was Mario Cuomo's address at the 1984 Democratic Convention in San Francisco. His brilliant speech delivered when most American homes were tuned in created instant name recognition for him, and he has since become a national figure who many had expected would run for president in 1988 or 1992.

The media, especially television, create name recognition, which is the first requirement of a successful campaign. With this much influence over public opinion, one would expect that television and the other media would exercise this influence more responsibly -- educating, informing and analyzing issues that are critical for the electorate to make informed and intelligent choices. But this is generally not the case.

In covering campaigns, especially presidential campaigns, television is largely interested in sensation and show business. The press concentrates on the strategic game played by the candidates in their pursuit of the presidency, thereby de-emphasizing questions of national policy and leadership. [30] Heavily emphasized are the simple mechanics of campaigning -- "the candidates' travels here and there, their organizational efforts, their strategies -- as well as voting projections and returns, likely conventions scenarios and so on." [31] Television, in particular, tends to focus on a candidate's image, form and symbolism rather than the substance.

In their well-rehearsed appearances, candidates are presented not in terms of their voting records on policy questions or their stands on various issues, but merely in terms of their ability to project a personal image of charm, warmth, youth, vigor, honesty, and integrity. By focusing primarily on these, the media ignore the important issues such as which candidate would make a better president, policy positions, personal leadership characteristics, and candidates' public and private histories.

As a result American politics has become a competition for images or between images rather than between ideals. All this has meant that "the three New York-based Networks, via their news and documentary programs, have become the arbiters of American opinion," declares Kevin Phillips. [32] Various survey results show that television has the greatest influence on public opinion in the United States. As Phillips states;

Wary as many are, however, citizens still expect the campaign to inform them, thereby putting the media in a position to influence their perceptions. What voters see in the newspaper and on television will affect what they *perceive* to be the important events, critical issues and serious contenders; it will affect what they learn about the candidates' personalities and issues and positions."[33] (emphasis mine)

Since voters' decisions may depend on what they *perceive* to be important and at stake when they make their choice, the influence of the media cannot be exaggerated. [34] Yet a major tenet of classical democracy theory requires that issues play the decisive role in electoral choice. The ideal citizen was one who based his or her decisions on the issues at hand and did not rely on "mere group attachment or partisan affiliations or candidate attractiveness as bases for electoral choices." [35]

I find it difficult, for example, to understand why an average voter in the United States can fall for any candidate who rehearses ten times for an interview, hires a media consultant to coach him about handling the media, and the television viewer, and hires a debate coach who teaches him, in advance, how to answer debate questions before making an appearance on television. My old-fashioned instincts tell me that honesty needs no rehearsing and that charm needs no coaching, that vigor and youth do not require ten coats of makeup, and that simple decency needs no practice.

In this quest for images the American election is trivialized to the extent that candidates will go out of their way to get it or apologize for the lack of it. After his debate with Walter Mondale in the 1984 presidential election, Reagan found it necessary to defend himself. He remarked, "If I had as much makeup as he [Mondale] did, I'd have looked younger too." I think this was an insult to the intelligence of the American voter. What did makeup have to do with the nuclear arms race, environmental pollution and degradation, the ever-increasing federal budget deficits, the high level of unemployment, and many other pressing problems in America?

In the United States, the artificial has become so commonplace that the natural sometimes seems to have been contrived. For example, given the opportunity to advise Senator Edward Kennedy on running for president, former President Richard Nixon, who had once blamed his makeup men for his loss of an election, offered, "Lose ten pounds."[36]   The implication: to make any serious and effective run for the White House, a candidate must look good. It has nothing to do with substance but style.

If this is all the advice that a former president who knows all the complexities of running a government can offer to a potential candidate, then it is not surprising that the American political process is in danger of becoming irrelevant to the nation's political and economic realities.   Realities such as increasing unemployment, crime, drugs, trade and budget deficits, the uncompetitive position of American producers, declining educational standards, environmental degradation, and a host of other problems beset the United States today.

But what else could the former president offer? The time-honored American marketplace of ideas that has been a hallmark of political discourse in the United States has largely been rendered obsolete by television with its one-second bytes. It has largely been replaced by a new metaphor, "the market place of images."

Can anyone imagine what the chances of the twenty-seventh president of the United States, William Howard Taft, a 300 pound heavyweight would be in today's American politics? How about the old Abe Lincoln, with his beard and melancholy face? Probably neither of these men would have much of a chance today! As Postman states, "In America God favors all those who possess both a talent and a format to *amuse*, whether they be preachers, athletes, entrepreneurs, *politicians,* or journalists."[37] (emphasis mine). In America, politics has become good looks and amiability, and certainly, not ideas.

This is as true in politics as much as it is in all other facets of American life. It explains why a basketball player can make over $10 million in one year and why an average doctor makes less than half a million dollars in a year. It also explains why American students always complain about a boring professor, and not a boring subject matter. A good professor must also be a good entertainer!

I realized the lack of attention to details in election coverage very early in my experience with American politics when Nixon ran against McGovern in 1972. I was then sympathetic to George McGovern and was very disappointed with the news media for failing to get what I believed were the important issues of the campaign to the American people so that they could make informed choices. I argued then that the television networks should devote more time to political news in addition to their standard thirty minutes allocated to the evening news.

After all, I argued, if most Americans depend on this medium to make their political choices, then they deserve to get more detailed analysis of the complex issues that face the nation rather than a projection of favorable images. I found the media to be interested only in talking about who was ahead in the polls, the strategies of candidates, campaign expenditures, and other issues that were useless in helping a voter make an informed and educated choice between candidates. Later, when the Watergate affair was exposed, I was not at all surprised.

I thought at the time that perhaps a little more probing and analysis of the various candidates' character, records, and backgrounds would have revealed not only Nixon's obsession with power, but also his potential to abuse his office and power. I also felt that the American press was not critical enough, especially in detecting the lies that are paraded in election campaigns as truths.

I found myself agreeing with what Walter Lippmann wrote in 1920: "There can be no liberty for a community which lacks the means by which to detect lies."[38] As it turns out, however, I discovered later that it was not the American press that was incapable of detecting lies. It was the public that had lost interest in politics and had grown apathetic. With an apathetic populace, politicians have been successful in saying as little as possible and, most importantly, staying away from controversial and difficult public policy issues.

In 1988, fewer than 10 percent of those voting in the presidential election felt that the candidates adequately addressed their concerns. More than 54 percent also believed that neither candidate talked enough about important national issues such as health, homelessness, education, the economy, and the budget deficit.[39]

Politicians now hire media consultants who advise them about specific images that can be marketed to the voters and issues that must be avoided. They help design campaigns filled with pretense and image projections, campaigns designed to avoid critical issues and instead to revolve around unassailable images of the day such as "candidates standing squarely behind flags, fetuses, bibles, and other images that move voters at deeper levels" and arouse passions rather than elicit objective assessments of facts and choices.[40]

But that is not all. Politicians are trying not only to avoid difficult issues and to control what they say to the voters, but also to control what the media reports. With the media assuming such a powerful position in politics, politicians are searching frantically for new techniques and are perfecting old ones to control them. Out of this search has emerged "the technology of media management, with its Orwellian vocabulary of spin doctors, damage control, sound bites, line of the day, and photo-opportunities, all orchestrated by ever-present handlers whose job is to keep reporters as far removed from spontaneous contact with the candidate as possible."[41]

The effect of this has been negative for the voter. It has made it increasingly difficult for voters to make the right choices and has contributed to the increasingly artificial nature of the American political process. Peggy Noonan, the former speech writer for President Reagan, captures the increasingly artificial process of the American political process when she states:

At the end of the Reagan era all the presidential candidates looked like TV news Guys.

At the end of the Reagan era they had all gone to the same TV coaches, and they all talked with their voices low and cool, . . . moving their hands within the same frame for emphasis, moving their hands the same way with studied, predictable natural mannerisms. . . Candidates with prefab epiphanies, inauthentic men for an inauthentic age.[42]

Perhaps politicians are not just inauthentic men and women, but rational individuals acting to maximize their reelection possibilities in a media controlled political game.   The media have the power to change voters' attitudes, perceptions, behavior, and public opinion.   This power was remarkably underscored in a poll that was conducted right after the first 1984 presidential debate between Ronald Reagan and Walter Mondale.   In a *New York Times*/CBS News poll of 329 voters taken immediately after the debate on Sunday night, 43 percent thought Mondale had won, while 34 percent judged Reagan the winner.   But after two days of press and television postmortems, 515 people responding to a similar poll by the same organization on Tuesday, awarded Mondale the victory by an overwhelming 66 percent to 17 percent.

Today, 41 percent of Americans feel that television has become too powerful in American society.   Many see the American public as having "become a plastic to be molded by the news media into any form they want, making the free and independent citizen beloved of democratic theorists an automaton actuated by impulses transmitted by anonymous rulers through the system of mass communication," thus rendering American democracy a mediacracy.

For the sake of American democracy and all others who look to the United States as a good example of a modern day pluralistic democracy, I hope things are not as bad as I have portrayed them in this chapter.

NOTES

1. "Democratic Strings," *West Africa*, June 25 - July 1, 1990, p. 1065.

2. See W. Lance Bennett, *The Governing Crisis* (New York: St. Martin's Press, 1992), p. 9.

3. Henry Cabot Lodge, ed., *The Federalist* (New York: Knickerbocker Press, 1895), p. 323.   Reprinted from Alexander Hamilton's original text.

4. Herbert Asher, *Presidential Elections and American Politics* (Homewood, IL.: Dorsey Press, 1976), p. 86.   Revisionist research since then has concluded that these findings were timebound.   For revisionist findings, see V. O. Key, Jr., *The Responsible Electorate* (New York: Vintage Books, 1966), p. 7;   David Repass, "Issues Salience and Party Choice," *American Political Science Review* 65 (June 1971): 390 - 394;   Samuel A. Kirkpatrick and Melvin E. Jones, "Issue Public and the Electoral System: The Role of Issues in Electoral Change," in *Allen R. Wilcox, ed., Public Opinion and Political Attitudes* (New York: John Wiley & Sons, 1974), pp. 537 - 555.

5. See Asher, *Presidential Elections and American Politics*, p.43.

6. Bennett, *The Governing Crisis,* p. 2.

7. Angus Campbell et al., *The American Voter* (New York: John Wiley & Sons, 1960), pp. 89 - 115.

8. See Bennett, *The Governing Crisis,* p. 15.

9. Kevin Phillips, "America, 1989: Brain-Dead Politics in Transition," *Washington Post*, reprinted in the *International Herald Tribune*, October 4, 1989, p. 8.

10. See Campbell et al., *The American Voter.* See also, David RePass's findings and other revisionists findings which contradict Campbell's findings. See note 3 above.

11. Revisionist research has concluded that these findings were time-bound. See note 8 above.

12. William Flanigan, *Political Behavior of the American Electorate* (Boston: Allyn & Bacon, Inc., 1968), p. 71.

13. See Walter de Vries, "American Campaign Consulting: Trends and Concerns," *PS: Political Science & Politics*, March 1989, pp. 21-25.

14. United States Information Agency, *What is Democracy* (Washington, D.C.: 1991), p. 16.

15. See de Vries, "American Campaign Consulting," pp. 21-25.

16. See Bennett, *The Governing Crisis*, p. 25.

17. See Campbell et al., *The American Voter,* pp. 89 - 115.

18. See Bennett, *The Governing Crisis,* p. 4.

19. Murray Edelman, *The Symbolic Uses of Politics* (Urbana: University of Illinois Press, 1970), p. 5.

20. Thomas E. Patterson, *The Mass Media Election* (New York: Praeger Publishers, 1980), p. 173.

21. Neil Postman, *Amusing Ourselves to Death* (New York: Penguin Books, 1986), p. 4.

22. John Drew, *Portrait of an Election: The 1980 Presidential Election* (New York: Simon & Schuster, 1981), p. 48.

23. See Postman, *Amusing Ourselves to Death,* p. 126.

24. Ibid., p. 156.

25. Edward Herman and Noam Chomsky, "Propaganda Mill," in George Mckenna and Stanley Fenigold, *Taking Sides* (Guilford, Conn.: Dushkin Publishing, 1993) p. 66.

26. V. O. Key, *Public Opinion and American Democracy* (New York: Knopf, 1961) p. 392. For the mirror analogy, see Sig Michelson, *The Electric Mirror* (New York: Dodd, Mead, 1972).

27. Paul Lazarsfeld, Bernard Berelson, and Hazel Gaudet, *The People's Choice,* 3rd ed. (New York: Columbia University Press, 1968). Originally published by Duell, Sloan and Pearce in 1944; Bernard Berelson, Paul Lazarsfeld, and William Mcphee, *Voting* (Chicago: University of Chicago Press, 1954).

28. From the earliest Gallup Polls in the mid-1930s until the early 1960s,

surveys indicated that 80 percent or more of the adult public identified with either the Republican or Democratic party. About half of these described themselves as strong partisans. Presently, however, party identifiers account for only about 60 percent of Americans, most of whom say they are weak partisans. See Patterson, *The Mass Media Election,* p. 5.

29. See Postman, *Amusing Ourselves to Death*, p. 132.

30. See Ibid., p. 21.

31. Ibid.

32. See Kevin Phillips, *Mediacracy* (Garden City, N.Y.: Doubleday, 1957), p. 28.

33. Ibid.

34. See Patterson, *The Mass Media Election*, p. 95.

35. See Asher, *Presidential Elections and American Politics*, p. 86.

36. See Postman, *Amusing Ourselves to Death*, p. 4.

37. Ibid., p. 5.

38. Ibid., p. 108.

39. Ibid., p. 25.

40. Ibid., p. 19.

41. Ibid., p. 6.

42. Ibid., p. 11.

Chapter 5

Political Corruption:
The American Style

In the previous chapter, I discussed the effect of the media on the U.S. political process. Clearly, one of the major effects of the media on the political process is increasing election spending, which has tended to confine political office to candidates who are independently wealthy, or are willing to sell their souls to political interest groups. The rich have taken over the American political process. The United States government that was once supposed to be "government of the people, for the people and by the people" has now become, as Walter Mondale puts it, "government of the rich, for the rich, and by the rich."

The 1982 midterm elections are a good example. In that year, two candidates spent $10 million each on their campaigns. In New York, Republican Lew Lerhman spent over $10 million of his own money to seek the governorship of the state, and in Texas, another Republican gubernatorial candidate spent more than $10 million of his own money. It was a year in which at least five House candidates broke, or came close to, the million dollar mark. Even more incredible were the cases where spending totaled more than $1 million in two state legislature races -- both for seats in the California legislature that pay $28,000 annually.

Today, statewide campaigns for governor or United States senator in an average-size state cost at least $2 million and have run as high as $10 million.[1] The high cost of campaigns reflects the new wave of campaigning which includes polling, direct mail solicitation and the increased expense of producing and showing quality political advertisements. A quality thirty-second spot commercial may cost $500,000 to produce and from $1,000 to $5,000 to show on a big-city television station. In presidential campaigns, a national network thirty-second spot on prime-time television may cost up to $100,000.

Common Cause, a public interest group lobby, estimated that Senate and House candidates spent roughly $300 million in 1982, up by 25 percent from 1980. This was expected to increase even further in 1984, and it did. In 1984, many candidates broke campaign spending records. For example, campaign expenditures for the 1984 presidential election totaled $325 million, $50 million more than in the previous election.[2] Spending on congressional elections also increased dramatically in subsequent years totaling $450 million in 1986, more than double the amount spent in 1978. Jay Rockefeller, for example, spent $9 million to win the Senate seat of tiny West Virginia (population approximately 1.5 million).

The question that needs to be asked is, "Can a candidate buy a public office?" The concern about this possibility was raised a long time ago by Richard Henry

Lee, a signatory of the Declaration of the Independence. Speaking for many of the Anti-Federalists and those who opposed the ratification of the Constitution, he warned that the proposed charter shifted power away from the people and into the hands of the "aristocrats and moneyites," those who "avariciously grasp at all power and property."

The evidence today, though not conclusive, suggests that Lee's fears were justified. Political candidates may be buying public offices. Lavish spending did buy offices in both 1982 and 1984. For example, Democratic businessman Frank Lautenberg concedes that he could not have upset Republican Congresswoman Millicent Fenwick for a New Jersey Senate seat if he had not spent over $5 million to Fenwick's $1.4 million. Fred Wertheimer of Common Cause declared after the 1982 elections: "Any one who argues that money was not a crucial factor in this election is not really looking at what happened."

My impression is that this increased election spending, more than anything else, is responsible for the high level of political corruption in American politics today. For example, to finance their increasing election spending, political candidates have turned to political action committees, also known as PACs. As a result of the influence of PACs, American politics has become as corrupt as politics anywhere in the developing world, if not worse.

The difference in political corruption in the United States and elsewhere is that political corruption in the United States is subtle, legal, and sophisticated. To deceive the masses, American politicians have coined new names for all the old corrupt practices, hoping to make corruption much more acceptable. For example, instead of calling the practice where politicians sell their consciences and positions for political contributions outright corruption, abuse of office, power, or public trust, they have chosen to call it interest group politics, lobbying, or influence peddling -- new names for old crimes. This is all done in an attempt to give corruption respectability and thus make it more appealing and acceptable.

For an African to speak out against corruption in the American politics is like living in a glass house and engaging in a stone-throwing contest. Yes, corruption is endemic in African politics, and this I condemn without any reservations. In my judgment, there is probably not a single African political leader today who is not corrupt. This is no secret. We have all read about African political leaders, especially the dictators among them -- Mobutu of Zaire, Moi of Kenya, Houphet of the Ivory Coast, Babaginda of Nigeria, just to name a few -- who have stashed millions and, in some cases, billions of dollars in Swiss banks, when their impoverished people struggle for food and other basic necessities of life.[3] Given the high level of poverty in Africa, it is clear that corruption, which diverts national resources from development projects, especially where they are stashed in overseas account, can impose tremendous hardship on an already impoverished people. I believe that the negative economic and social effects of corruption are much more pervasive in Africa than in the United States. Therefore, my attack on political corruption in the United States is by no means designed to *endorse* the practice in Africa or anywhere else for that matter. It is only a reflection of my disappointment with the American political system, as much as I am equally disgusted and repulsed by the political corruption in Africa.

After all, Americans have often associated corruption with underdevelopment. It has been argued that people from the developing countries are more disposed to become corrupt because of poverty, and thus, if for no other reason at all, it is a means to supplement the meager "legally" earned incomes from work. For many public officials corruption is viewed as a means to make ends meet. Another reason why Americans have tended to view corruption as associated with the developing world is that, in most of these countries, the laws are so poorly enforced, and power so personalized, that the probability of being caught, prosecuted, and actually punished for corruption is so low that there is a great incentive to be corrupt. The argument has nothing to do with any inherent human weaknesses in people from the developing world, as much as it has to do with the legal and institutional systems that make corruption a much riskier enterprise in the United States than in the developing world. For these reasons, an individual in a developing country is more willing to risk being caught, and he is therefore more likely to engage in some kind of corrupt activity.

To the average American, corruption tends to have a foreign connotation -- an association with a Third World dictator. Their favorite whipping boys are the Marcoses of the Philippines, the Duvaliers of Haiti, Mobutu of Zaire, the shah of Iran, and Moi of Kenya -- who ironically were all good friends of the United States at one time and squander U.S. taxpayers' money intended for their impoverished people. While the Americans' association of corruption with the developing world may be true to some extent, political corruption and abuse are not necessarily limited to the developing world.

My research into the U.S. political system reveals an astonishing level of corruption among its politicians. Add nepotism, cronism, and influence peddling to political corruption in the United States, and you have some of the worst political abuses that Americans have generally associated have only with the developing countries. Political corruption in the United States would make instant headlines in the news if it is happening in another country, especially in an African country.

What may be called corruption and abuse of public trust in Africa and other parts of the developing world, Americans will refer to as influence peddling or lobbying. What may be called tribal politics and nepotism in African politics, Americans will explain away casually as nonexistent in their democratic political culture. After all, Americans argue that there are no tribes in the United States, and how can a nation without tribal affiliations play tribal politics? They will thus argue that in a civilized country people are appointed to higher positions, based not on a flimsy concept such as tribalism, but on their competence, or something more objective than a subjective tribal loyalty. Thus, an American president appoints people to positions not because they are from his tribe, but because they are his friends, brothers, relatives, and in many cases from his home state. Tribal politics? No, only regional politics! Crony politics? No, only Marcos had cronies; crony politics is practiced only in the underdeveloped world!

Americans have been very innovative. By providing new names for known political abuses, politicians and the American public at large have deluded themselves into believing that they do not have any of the political problems in the developing countries -- political corruption, nepotism, cronism, and many others. However, a survey of the facts shows otherwise.

First, let's look at what Americans call lobbying. Lobbying is defined by my American Heritage dictionary as, "to seek to influence legislation." While lobbying may not in itself be considered a corrupt practice, the mechanism by which this influence is obtained generally borders on corruption. Lobbying has become the most powerful technique of interest groups -- direct attempts to influence legislation and political elections through donations, contributions, and contacts with politicians. By so doing, the lobbyist attempts to "subvert" the political process and the "integrity of the politician." This is certainly one kind of corruption. In fact, my dictionary defines corruption as "an attempt to subvert or destroy the honesty and integrity of someone." As the two definitions of (lobbying and corruption) make clear, there may indeed be a fine line between lobbying and corruption of public officials. However, my observation is that the lobbyists have frequently crossed this line with impunity.

Lobbyists have always operated in Washington, but they have never been as many and as influential, their activity so legitimized and their efforts so publicized. What used to be viewed as "somewhat a shady, and relatively disreputable trade" has "burst onto the American scene with a high degree of respectability" and acceptance. Motivated by the staggering fees lobbyists can command, lawmakers and their aides are quitting their jobs to join lobbying firms in order to cash in on their connections. For some of these public officials, public service has become an apprenticeship for a more lucrative career as a special interest lobbyist.

Lobbying today is one of the fastest growing industries in the America. The number of registered lobbyists has more than doubled since 1976, from 3,420 to 8,800 in 1984. In 1992, there were about 4,100 PACs in the United States, with more than one hundred new PACs being formed each year.[4] In 1985 as many as two hundred retired congressmen represented clients around the capital.[5] Today, PACs represent every political interest, sometimes working for two opponents at the same time.

The question is, What do people who hire lobbyists get for their money? Why do individuals in a democracy have to hire a lobbyist to get the politicians to do what they want? It seems to me that the will of the people is registered through free and open election, which is granted to all free people in a democratic political system. It appears to me an indictment of the democratic process, if having voted for a politician, a voter then has to hire a lobbyist to get the politician to fulfil his election promises or save the interest of the electorate. This sounds rather strange and quite un-American.

Perhaps these lobbyists may not be trying to get the politician to serve the interests of their constituents, as much as to protect the narrow and selfish interests of lobbyist and big business over the national and the public interest. Indeed, with few exceptions, PACs are formed not to pursue a certain principle but to protect the narrowest of special interests. It is obvious that PACs will not give money if they do not get the desired results. As former Senator Paul Laxalt put it, "Everybody needs a Washington *Representative* to protect their hindsides, even foreign governments" (emphasis mine).   Unfortunately, I will have to disagree with the honorable senator.

I thought that when individuals voted in an election, they were voting for their *representatives* in Washington! Why do they need a hired gun to represent them? And what happened to the representative government deriving its just powers from the governed? The reality is that the senator is right. As former senator Gary Hart of Colorado told the United States Senate:

It seems the only group without a well-heeled PAC is the average citizen -- the voter who has no special interest beyond low taxes, an efficient government, an honorable Congress, and a humane society. Those are the demands we should be heeding -- but those are the demands the PACS have drowned.[6]

But some observers have argued that since PACs also represent some of the governed, and their activities are a normal part of the democratic process. Again, I disagree with this line of reasoning. In a democracy, any principles or rules that permit inequalities in influence for whatever reasons -- superior wisdom or greater wealth -- should be recognized as antidemocratic. [7]

It is reasonable to argue that the successes of the civil rights movement and the white backlash, the loss of the Vietnam War, corruption in Washington, and the prolonged economic recession of the 1970s, all set the stage for Reagan's election in 1980.   In office however, the Reagan era brought about an unprecedented level of corruption. Indeed, he lost a significant number of his aides to special interest lobbying groups. None was more successful, at least for some time, than Reagan's former deputy chief of staff and longtime California friend, Micheal Deaver.   Deaver successfully multiplied his White House income sixfold only a year after leaving government service.

Other Reagan aides who peddled their influence after leaving government service include Kenneth Duberstein, Lynn Nofziger and Ed Rollins.   By representing clients like the Teamsters Union, Rollins, for example, who never earned more than $75,000 in government, made as much as ten times the amount he earned while in office. These former administration officials were often paid millions of dollars by special interest groups to oppose policies that the officials once ardently supported or even helped shaped while in government.   This is particularly true in the area of foreign trade, as documented by a *Washington Post* article that appeared in March 1986. In this particular case, Reagan had ordered an investigation into the unfair trade practices of South Korea. Ironically, that country was at the same time paying Reagan's former deputy chief of staff, Deaver, $1.2 million over a period of three years to "protect, manage, and expand trade and economic interests" of South Korea. To do this job, Deaver turned around and hired Doral Cooper, a former deputy trade representative in the Reagan administration to help him. For South Korea it was a simple, logical step to take: if you want somebody to unravel something, who can do it better than the person who raveled it in the first place? Is at all surprising that less than a few months after leaving office, President Reagan himself joined what his aides before him had done and went to Japan on a $7 million promotional tour sponsored by a Japanese firm, Fujisankei Communication Group. Reagan personally pocketed $2 million for his nine-day cameo appearances. [8]

I am sure there are many Americans who will argue that what I have described above does not constitute political corruption or abuse of public trust or privilege. But I dare to hope that these individuals will agree with me, whatever their feelings are, that the above cannot be considered proud features of the American political system.

Nevertheless, two of the important things that should be of great concern to everyone are: What are these lobbyists selling, and why is the influence of lobbyists on the American political system bad? The first concern has partially been addressed earlier. The lobbyists are selling nothing more than their connections and influence in government. What has become a new feature of the U.S. political system and is appropriately referred to as the revolving-door system was particularly pronounced in the Reagan era.

But Micheal Deaver, Kenneth Duberstein, Lynn Nofziger, and Ed Rollins were not the only ones who left the Reagan administration to cash in on their connection. There were many more, all eager to cash in on their access to the Reagan White House. As Deaver put it himself, "I have as much access as anybody." A few of these aides were;

- ●Richard Allen, former national security adviser
- ●Lee Atwater, former White House aide
- ●Joseph Canzeri, former White House assistant to Michael Deaver
- ●Robert Gray, 1981 Reagan co-chairman for the inauguration.
- ●Christopher Lehman, former National Security Council staff member
- ●Daniel Murphy, Vice-president Bush's former chief of staff
- ●Nancy Reynolds, Reagan's confidante and transition official
- ●Richard Schweiker, former secretary for human and health services.

The list could fill many more pages. These, and many more, were selling their connections in government. As the lobbyist Frank Mankiewicz bluntly puts it, "I will tell you what we're selling. The return phone call."

The second question I posed above was, why do individuals in a democracy have to hire lobbyist to get their politicians to do what they want? To answer this second question, one needs to know what the objectives of those who hire these lobbyist are, as well as how the actions and activities of the lobbyists affect the political process and the national interest in general. It is no secret that many well-intentioned congressional reforms have been subverted by the activities of lobbyists who have attempted to exploit the spiraling cost of election spending to keep congressmen and women hostages to special interest groups. The effect of this has been nothing more than institutional paralysis. W. Lance Bennett argues that "PAC pressures undermine institutional support for governing ideas."[9] A good example is the fact that Congress and the Reagan administration actually had to go along with an unprecedented measure, the Gramm-Rudman automatic trigger measure designed to balance the budget. The reason why that measure was grudgingly accepted was that no one in Congress seemed to have the guts to cut spending or raise taxes. It was much easier to have an automatic trigger to do that rather than to be identified as the one who did it! Is this a copout?

Another example is the Reagan tax bill. Reagan had put the prestige of his office and his personal appeal behind the bill and had gone out to the people to promote it. At one time, Reagan referred to the bill and its passage as "a test of the supreme interest of the people against special interest groups." I was actually not too surprised when it was revealed that President Reagan was indeed not fighting against just any special interest groups, but special interest groups that had hired some of his own former aides who may have helped shape the bill, which they were now working to defeat. In appealing for public support for his bill, the president accused those special interest groups that opposed him as "swarming like ants through every nook and cranny of Congress." I am sure Reagan knew very well that many of those ants were there because of their connection to him.

Some political and social scientists, subscribing to the pluralistic view of America, have argued that in a pluralistic society each group has a tendency to counterbalance the power of others. Thus, no single group can dominate the political system or have a monopoly of power. They argue in effect that interest group politics are a normal part of the American democratic process. I suspect that they may even want to extend the argument to Adam Smith's concept of the enlightened self-interest. They will then argue that, like capitalism, by serving their own clients' interest, lobbyists may end up serving the interest of society as a whole.

The facts that I have uncovered in my research on this topic have led me to conclude that objectives that are usually pursued by lobbyists are many times inimical to society's interest. Thus, the assertions above are not generally true. For one thing, group interests are generally very narrow and, more often than not, opposed to the public interest. Many who argue in favor of interest group politics do not realize that the traditional representative of the electorate in Washington has now been bought by these groups and that the average American no longer has a representative in Washington. The few "traditional representatives" who have not been bought yet are equally afraid of the power of special interest groups, so that they stay away from or avoid controversial issues that can arouse the anger of the lobbyists. In fact, Bennett attributes the low voter interest in politics to the lack of ideas that would interest them because many of those ideas "have already been bought and taken off the market by political action committees (PACs) and other political investors who finance candidates." [10]

This fear of the special interest group was manifestly demonstrated in Washington when a measure designed to curtail the influence of special interest groups was introduced in the House. This bill upon passage would have limited campaign contributions by special interest groups. Not surprisingly, this bill did not get too far. By a vote of 84 to 7, the Senate opted to study the bill further. Senators may have reasoned that by hamstringing the special interest groups, they would be killing the goose that laid the golden egg, thus denying themselves not only the sources of their campaign funds, but also the advantage of incumbering over potential challengers. The money from PACs helps to keep incumbents in office.

Every political system needs to be continually infused with new blood, new perspectives, and a renewed sense of urgency in dealing with national problems. For a very long time all of us, and especially the United States, ridiculed the former Soviet Union and Chinese political systems as being dominated by old men with old ideas, people who had lost touch with new realities and perspectives about international political and social change. Today, however, in the United States Congress can be found people whose tenure in Congress stretches into several decades, many made possible by the funds provided by PACs. The activities of PACs and other big business lobbyists have made it nearly impossible to defeat an incumbent politician they support in the United States.

In 1991 - 1992, PACs dished out $205 million in special interest contributions to favored legislators and political parties. Nearly $189 million, or 92 percent, went to congressional candidates, with *three-fourths* of the money going to incumbents and only one-fourth to challengers. [11] Does this deliberate attempt to keep the incumbents already doing the "bidding" of lobbyists in Congress, rather than bringing in new faces, new ideas, and new blood into the political process, pose serious ethical and credibility problems for American democracy?

In another instance, in 1980, a powerful conservative political action committee, the National Conservative Political Action Committee (NCPAC), distributed to voters in five states little cards with the words "Target 80" written beneath them. The cards were directed against the so-called super-liberal Democratic senators -- Alan Cranston of California, George McGovern of South Dakota, Birch Bayh of Indiana, John Culver of Iowa, and Frank Church of Idaho. All five were the targets of intensive campaigns waged by NCPAC. By election day, NCPAC had spent $2.8 million. And what were the results of the effort and spending of NCPAC? You can guess, all the targeted candidates but Cranston of California lost the election.

The close correlation between special interest donations and the way American lawmakers vote gives the appearance that the entire United States Congress is for sale. This certainly creates credibility problems for Congress. Senator Bob Dole, the Republican Minority leader states: "When these PACS give money, they expect something in return other than good government. It is making it difficult to legislate. We may reach a point where everybody is buying something with PAC money. *We cannot get anything done*"[12] (emphasis mine). In other words, activities of PACs have directly contributed to the institutional paralysis that we see in Washington. Former Democratic Congressman Thomas Downey of New York, is even more blunt, "You can't buy a Congressman for $5,000. But you can buy his vote. It's done on a regular basis." Examples of the Congressman Downey's indictment of Congress are plentiful. A few of these are as follows:

The Professional Bill. The American Medical Association (AMA), and Dental Association have been lobbying for a law that would exempt professionals from Federal Trade Commission's regulation, and thus permit them to fix their prices. While the bill was awaiting House action, the two groups gave over $2.3 million to House members, 72 percent of it to the 213 co-sponsors of the bill. Each sponsor of the bill received an average of $7,598. According to Ralph Nader's Congress Watch, Thomas Luken, the prime sponsor of the bill, received $14,750.

The Beer Bill. Brewers want to be allowed to designate monopoly territories for their distributors, which could raise the cost of beer by 20 percent. Meanwhile, the SIXPAC, the beer lobby, handed out $350,000 to members of the Judiciary Subcommittees on Monopolies. Democrat Jack Brooks of Texas, the chief sponsor of the bill, got $10,000 from the PAC.

The Bankruptcy Bill. A bill that would require individuals and not businesses to pay back debts after declaring bankruptcy was pending before the House. Six Credit PACs, led by the American Bankers Association, and Household Finance Corp., meanwhile donated over $700,000 to 255 Congressmen who were co-sponsoring the bill. These and many more of the activities of the special interest group indicate that their interest may not necessarily converge with the national interest. [13]

Even though PACs can give no more than $5,000 to a single candidate, and contributions are filed with the Federal Election Commission, their influence on the political process is very significant. Former Congressman Leon Panetta of California, now President Clinton's Chief of Staff, attested to the influence of PACs: "There is a danger that we are putting ourselves on the auction blocks every day. It's now tough to hear the voices of the citizens in your district. Sometimes the only things you can hear are the loud voices in three-piece suit carrying a PAC check."

Edward Roeder, a compiler of a directory called PAC American, referring

to the fact that some congressmen may have been bought by PACs, stated:
"Many seats have been bought but not paid for. We will see whether they are
put up for sale," Fred Wertheimer, president of Common Cause, also believes
that "our system of representative government is under siege because of the
destructive role that political action committees or PACs are now playing in our
political system."

In America today, it has become standard procedure for a rich candidate to
lend huge sums of money to his campaign from his personal fortune and then
stage fund-raising parties after the election at which he solicits funds from PACs
to repay himself. Again, this method of soliciting funds provides too much
accessibility, and indeed, increases the potential exposure of an elected
representative to sell himself to the PACs and other lobbyists. It certainly
cannot be viewed as a normal functioning of the democratic process.

Lobbying gets really nasty when serving congressmen find themselves being
lobbied by their former colleagues who have become hired guns to help change
laws that they may have worked hard to pass when they served in government.
More than two hundred former congressmen and women have stayed in
Washington, D.C., after leaving office, to represent special interest groups,
sometimes lobbying on the same legislation that they had helped draft and pass
into law. My question is, Have these honorable congressmen and women
suddenly realized that they passed bad laws, and now want them changed, or
have they been paid to change their minds and the minds of their colleagues?

The seriousness of lobbying by former congressmen and women must be
viewed with respect to their accessibility to the centers of power. Former
congressmen and women are free to go onto the floor of Congress and into the
cloakrooms,even though they are not supposed to lobby there. "Well, they don't
call it lobbying." says Senator David Pryor of Arkansas. "They call it visiting.
But you know exactly what they're there for." Former lawmakers have similar
access to the White House, and they use this access to serve the interests of their
clients.

Americans can call these practices any name they want -- special interest
politics, sleazy politics, pork-barrel politics, crony politics, favoritism, or
nepotism -- the fact remains that corruption is widespread in American politics
and poses a major threat to the American political system which both
theoretically and in practice must grant equal access and one man one vote to
each and every citizen. Today, there are many who exercise more than one vote
and have unlimited access to power, particularly where it counts most!

A top presidential aide, later to become United States attorney general, the
nation's chief law enforcement officer, with over seventeen years of friendship
with President Reagan, takes a personal loan from a friend. Twenty-two days
after the loan, on which he paid no interest, the lender gets a federal
government job paying him $59,000 annually. A few months later, this man's
wife also gets a federal government job that pays her over $30,000 annually.
Three others who helped the attorney general financially are all handsomely

rewarded with important federal government jobs. Is this corruption? No; according to American laws, these are merely unethical behaviors but not illegal. But are a political system and the people who run it corrupt if they shelter high government officials from being prosecuted when they abused their office and public trust? Is a political system that places some individuals in society above the law not corrupt?

Former CIA director William Casey was accused of misleading investors about his financing of a New Orleans Agribusiness Company. He sailed through the investigation without a scratch. No big deal, he had broken no laws. His actions were merely unethical! Similarly, a top aide to President Reagan, Max Hugel, was accused of illegal stock manipulations. Under pressure, he quit government as a free man. The argument was that he did not actually commit any serious crime, his actions were merely improper, unethical, and immoral. Prosecuted? No, there is not enough evidence for him to be prosecuted.

While serving as the U.S. attorney general in the Reagan administration, William French Smith took a whopping tax deduction ($66,000) for a $16,000 investment. When caught, he agreed to reduce the deduction to avoid prosecution. His action was defended as being only unethical but not a violation of the law.

Similarly, Deputy Secretary of Defense Paul Thayer, also in the Reagan administration, accused of insider trading, resigned his office. Prosecuted? No, his actions were only unethical.

For these same crimes, thousands are going to jail in America everyday. And for much lesser crimes, blacks, the poor, and other minorities are being sent to jails all across the country. Double standard in justice? But this is nothing new in the United States, I am told. The American justice appears to always work against the poor, the minority, and the social underclass.

The cases cited above are generally referred to in American politics as "sleazy factors" that are mere political inconvenience. I, however, don't see them that way. I view them as abuse of office, public trust, and privilege. I also believe that these individuals should not be let off the hook to enjoy their booty but, rather, should be punished. Even more importantly, a political system that allows such individuals to go away as free men is itself corrupt.

One can easily fill a whole book with these "sleazies." In 1984, Gary Hart, then a presidential candidate, released a list of fifty five top officials in the Reagan administration who faced "serious allegations of wrongdoing involving unethical behavior, abuse of power, or privilege, or even in some cases, criminal actions." He charged that "Abuses of Government have become a way of life in this administration, yet it seems to concern no one very much -- not even the President. It should."

I believe that history will judge the Reagan years as an era that legitimized political greed and corruption and lent respectability and acceptance to the two. It will be viewed as the era that brought into full bloom the "me generation," a generation that was committed to looking after its own interest in disregard of society's overall interests. For this group, everything was evaluated on the basis of "what's in it for me?" It surely was an era during which business, especially defense contractors, were overbilling, overcharging, and over-invoicing the Defense Department. It was also the era when more Americans sold national security information to United States' adversaries for a buck. It was an era that brought the political alienation that began in the 1960s and pushed along by the Watergate scandal, to a full circle.

The ethical laxity that has become a permanent feature of the American political system, especially as it was manifested during the Reagan years, and the blatant attempts to favor the rich over the poor in Reagan's economic policies, seriously challenge the American concept of participatory democracy, which supposedly provides equal access, justice, opportunity, and government for all the people, and not for only some of the rich. One of the key characteristics of participatory democracy is the continued responsiveness of government to the preferences of all its citizen, not just some of the citizens.

Many, including Walter Mondale, former vice president, and the Democratic presidential candidate of 1984, have accused the Reagan administration of being a government of the rich, by the rich, and for the rich. There may be some truth in this allegation. President Reagan, at the time he was in office was worth in excess of $5 million. His chief of staff, Donald Regan, was worth over $20 million, and there were perhaps more millionaires in the Reagan administration than in any other administration in American history. But this by itself is not enough to make a government one of the rich and for the rich. I believe the administration should be judged on the basis of its policies, and their effects on the country, rather than on the basis of the number of millionaires that shaped its policies. But what does the Reagan record show? In his first "royal coronation," Reagan and his rich friends treated the wealthy and lucky Americans who managed to get the royal invitation to a nouveau-riche extravaganza that cost the taxpayer an unprecedented inauguration expense of $16.3 million. As a seasoned politician remarked at the time, "the inauguration balls, the limousines, and the all-night dinner parties were symbolic of the kind of people who were about to take over the presidency of the United States." The second inauguration was supposed to be a scaled down version of the first. It was also billed: "We the people . . . An American celebration." It cost U.S. taxpayers $10 million.

While the "people's celebration" was going on, millions of homeless Americans, some sleeping on the streets only one block from the White House, were freezing in the extraordinary cold winter weather of that day! I suppose hardly any common person could be found at any of the galas and balls of that day. Similarly, I suspect it was difficult to find any of America's poor riding in any of the two hundred limousines that were rented for the occasion.

But that was not all. At the time when Mrs. Reagan was buying china for $209,000 and getting Mr. Reagan's rich friends to pay $800,000 for the redecoration of his private room in the White House, there were millions of

Americans who could not find a place to sleep, much less find food to put on any china.

In contrast, at his inaugural in 1976 President Carter did not advertise any people's celebration. He showed how a people's celebration could be organized. He did it when he broke tradition and walked all the distance on Pennsylvania Avenue to the site of his inauguration. He did it when he spent less than half of the amount Reagan spent on his people's celebration, when he had less than one-half of the galas that Reagan had. By his actions rather than his words, he made the common person part of the celebration.

However, it may not be the extravagance of the Reagan era that bothers many people as much as the president's policies that tended to favor the rich at the expense of the poor. During Reagan's first term of office, the percentage of American children living in poverty went up from 17.9 percent to 21 percent. The number of Americans living below the official poverty level also increased by 34 percent.[14]

President Reagan's economic policies, cynically called Reaganomics, was seen by many as a windfall for the rich and wealthy. The nonpartisan Congressional Budget Office reported that from 1984 through 1985, an estimated *1.4* million households with incomes of $80,000 or more received tax reductions that totaled *$35.4* billion; over the same period, more than *40* million households that earned $20,000 or less received tax reductions worth only *$23.4* billion. A 400-page report published by the Urban Institute, "The Reagan Record," indicated that the president's policies had resulted in a $25 billion income transfer from the less worthy to the wealthiest one-fifth in this country. Thus, the erosion of economic power of those at the bottom half of the economic spectrum resulted from shifts in tax and spending policies during the Reagan era. These accounted for significant losses of income for every income group except the affluent.[15]

But if you were not one of the Reagan's rich friends, or a beneficiary of the nefarious activities of the PACs, you did not have to lose hope yet. Of course, since there are no tribes in the United States, the next best thing to do may be to locate an influential government official who comes from your home state.

In the United States, as in Africa and elsewhere, who you know can help open a lot of doors. Tommy Boggs was a highly successful lobbyist in Washington, D.C., during the Reagan years. He had among other things, family ties that many Americans may not have. For example, Tommy's mother, Lindy, was a congresswoman from Louisiana, and his father, the late Hale Boggs had been the House majority leader; these connections have not hurt his lobbying business. Other congressional families who as lobbyists have traded on their names for various interest groups include House Speaker Tip O'Neill's son, Kip; Senate Majority Leader Robert Dole's daughter, Robin; Senator Paul Laxalt's daughter Michelle; and House Appropriations Committee Chairman Jamie Whittens's son, Jamie, Jr. Can we call this a normal functioning of a democratic process?

A growing cottage industry in the lobbying field is helping congressmen and women to get elected through lobbying firms. This arrangement is designed basically to ingratiate the elected congressman or woman to the lobbyist and to allow him to later collect his IOUs. Many high-powered lobbying firms such as Black, Manafort, and Stone have taken not only to raising money for political candidates but actually to planning and running their campaigns: devicing strategies, wooing the media, and conducting polls. These firms get paid by the candidates for electioneering services, and also get paid by their clients to lobby these same candidates after they help them get elected. Some call this cozy arrangement "double dipping." I call it political corruption! Representative Andrew Jacobs of Indiana agrees. He states: "the only reason it isn't considered bribery is that congress gets to define bribery."[16]

Many Americans have become so obsessed with themselves that they can't imagine anything wrong with their system of government. They have grown so complacent from their material successes that they tend to forget how their freedoms were won. In their complacency, they make it a habit to brag and to ridicule others who are suffering from problems that they have plenty of in their own country. Take the case of an African dictator who shoots his way to power. This guy is not responsible to anyone. After all, he has imposed his will on his people. He has no national mandate, and his allegiance is only to his family, and sometimes to his tribe. This dictator sets out to form a government. He appoints his brother to a high-level post in government, his brother-in-law to a similar important post, and his clansmen to other important positions.

Obviously, the people in this impoverished country are angry, and legitimately so. But they have no means to change this government, and even if they do, they may be afraid of the price of an unsuccessful attempt to change the government. For most of these people, a tribal government, or for that matter, a government made up of family members is absolutely unacceptable!

In Africa this government and the politics of it would be called tribal politics, and it would be unacceptable, even if it could not be changed for the sake of fear. In the Philippines, Americans generally call this "crony politics." Americans, however, would contend that this kind of arrangement is impossible in their country, and if it happens at all it would be only an aberration. For Americans, this kind of politics does not exist because they do not have dictators. Since there are no tribes in the United States, there cannot be tribal politics. Yes, I acknowledge, for example, that President Reagan was democratically elected in a nation without tribes, but the nation has fifty different states. I have sometimes wondered if it is only by chance that Reagan was from California, and his secretaries of state, defense, justice, and interior were all from California. His chief of staff, and many of the most important positions in his administration, were also held by Californians. But this is not tribalism, of course not. I thought, perhaps, stateism? But I checked my dictionary, and obviously there is nothing like stateism!

I am told that in the United States appointments to high positions in government are based largely on merit. Thus President Kennedy appointed his thirty four-year-old brother United States attorney general, only on the basis of his merit and merit alone. The case of Bobby Kennedy has largely been dismissed as an aberration anyway. But how about the Georgia mafia that President Jimmy Carter brought with him to Washington? If I am not mistaken, most of them were from Georgia! In the United States, no one worries about these things, except when it occurs in an underdeveloped country. Americans tend to explain these things casually away: after all, the president needs to have around him, people he knows well and can trust! The African dictator justifies his tribalistic tendencies using the same argument.

But Americans are a civilized people, and they will never base their decisions on any important issue on irrational feelings such as like tribalism or "stateism." It is thus by chance that when Reagan ran against Walter Mondale in the 1984 presidential election, Mondale managed to win in only one state, and none other than his native Minnesota. What a nice coincidence! I suppose it is only by chance that in all the six presidential elections that I have witnessed in the United States, only one candidate had lost in his native state. Perhaps there is something of an affinity between the American concept of a "favorite son" and the African "tribal affinity."

I am also hardly convinced that it is only by chance that President Reagan was from California, that his secretaries of state and defense were also from California, and that California ended up attracting the greatest number of Pentagon dollars during the Reagan years. Yes, I know that a lot of the defense contractors are located in California. These industries have always been in California, but California has not always attracted the most defense contracts.

Political corruption, tribalism, nepotism, crony politics, abuse of office, public trust, and privilege are negative political terms that have become synonymous with politics in the developing world. However, if Americans were less apathetic and a little less complacent about the infallibility of their political systems, they would have long ago discovered that many of the political problems in the developing world have infested their own political system.

I think the American political system and government are heading toward an end that many of the Founding Fathers of the United States may never have imagined in their wildest dream: "Government of the rich, for the PACs, and controlled by the media." Southerners have a saying: "Don't fix it, if it ain't broke." I concede that the American political system "ain't broke" yet, but it is close and must be fixed before it actually falls apart. After all, America is too young to die!

NOTES

1. W. Lance Bennett, *The Governing Crisis* (New York: St. Martin's Press, 1992), p. 18

2. Ibid., p. 17

3. Zairean President Mobutu Sese Seko, for example is thought to be one of the richest men in the world, with estimated wealth reaching as high as $5 billion while the average Zairian make less than $200 per year. See *Wall Street Journal*, April 9, 1990, p. B5

4. George Mckenna and Stanley Feingold, *Taking Sides* (Guilford, Conn.: The Dushkin Publishing Group, Inc., 1993) p. 46

5. *TIME*, January 28, 1985 p. 44

6. Fred Wertheimer, "Campaign Finance Reform: The Unfinished Agenda," in *Taking Sides*, ed. George Mckenna and Stanley Feingold (Guilford, Conn.: The Dushkin Publishing Group, Inc., 1993) p. 49

7. Benjamin Page, *Choices and Echoes in Presidential Elections* (Chicago: University of Chicago Press, 1978) p. 10

8. See Bennett, p. 3

9. Ibid., p. 54

10. Ibid., p. 17

11. *Newsweek*, May 24, 1993, p. 6

12. Quoted in Bennett, p. 55

13. Bennett, p. 62

14. See *Wall Street Journal*, June 13, 1986, p. 48

15. Thomas Byrne Edsall, *Atlantic Monthly*, June 3, 1988, Reprinted in *The Future and the Individual*, ed. Mark West (Acton, Mass.: Copley Publishing Group, 1990)

16. Gary C. Jacobson, "Money in the 1980 and 1982 Congressional Elections," in *Money and Politics in the United States:* Financing Elections in the 1980s, edited by Michael J. Morbin (Washington, D.C.: American Enterprise Institute, Chatham House, 1984), p. 41

Chapter 6

Black Is Black

"We hold these truths to be
self evident that all men
are created equal."

It was September 5, 1972. I was dressed and ready to go to school. I was quite excited and yet very apprehensive. I had been in Albany, Oregon, for approximately two months. However, I had not seen a black person in this city of some forty thousand people. As a matter of fact, I had not even been conscious of my color. After all, I had been around people whom I trusted and who cared greatly. But today, I would be leaving the security of these kind people, to be thrown to perhaps an unkind world out there. I had been told that I would be the only black student at South Albany High School. This did not bother me; in fact, I had not thought much about it before.

My first day at school was uneventful. Earlier I had taken note of what many had pointed out rather reluctantly to me, "You have an accent," a fact that I continue to be reminded of after over two decades in the United States. I was, however, disappointed by the students apparent naivete about Africa and about the rest of the world. Prior to my arrival at South, there had been several newspaper articles about Ghana and Africa that were designed to familiarize the students with my country and the African continent in general. However, it appeared that these articles did nothing to improve the geography or the general knowledge of most of the students. Upon my arrival, very few knew about Africa, and fewer yet about Ghana. The kinds of questions these students asked, good as their intentions were, were most often offensive and insulting.

In many cases, more than anything else, they revealed a great deal of ignorance about modern Africa, but, even more importantly, they demonstrated at least an honest attempt to learn something about Africa. For example, many of the students still believed that most Africans roamed naked in the jungles, fighting each other with bows and arrows, sometimes eating each other according to the Darwinian theory of the survival of the fittest. I quickly welcomed this lack of knowledge about Africa as both a personal challenge and as an opportunity to help educate young American students. I vowed to myself that before I left the United States, I would do my level best to educate them about my country.

This resolution did not reduce my personal disappointment with their ignorance about Ghana and Africa, nor with the America's educational curricula which completely ignored teaching American students about the non-European world and culture. I was disappointed because students in Africa are required by the school authorities to take Western history, geography, politics, and literature very seriously in their studies. It appeared to me then (a feeling later to be confirmed) that many Americans had neither the interest nor the desire to learn about Africa. This initial assessment was increasingly proved correct as I dealt with college students, and even with professionals in the United States.

I began to understand why I had been in the United States for months and yet had heard nothing about Africa on the American news. This was to hold true throughout my stay in the United States. The American news media ignores Africa, and thus for months there may not be any substantive news about Africa. During my early days in America, most of the time that I heard anything about Africa on the news, it was invariably about some natural or man-made disaster, civil war, political corruption, or coup d'etat that had taken place somewhere in Africa. Eventually, I understood literally that no news about Africa really meant good news for Africa!

I quickly rationalized that perhaps Americans had realized their ignorance about Africa, and for that reason they had brought me here to help them learn about my country. For this reason, I felt an even greater sense of responsibility, not only to myself, the American Field Service program that brought me to the United States, and Ghana, but also to the entire people of Africa to represent the very best in Africa. I was not about to take any chance with this important assignment.

I was therefore very disappointed when I later found out that many students had believed two outrageous stories that I had told them about Africa. I had been kidding some friends that Africans lived on tree tops and that the American ambassador in Ghana indeed lived on the tallest tree in the capital with his family. At another time, I had told my friends that my family lived with animals and that I kept a pet elephant in our bath tub. These are jokes that practically every African who comes to America tells to blunt the American perception that Africans are primitive people.

I was soon aware that the story had made the rounds throughout the school and was moving through the city. Incredible as I thought the joke was, many people had believed it. After all, this was coming from the horse's own mouth. To them, I was merely confirming what they had already seen on their television sets when they watched the Tarzan movies, as well as what they had been reading in their textbooks. When I found out that they actually believed these stories, I realized the magnitude of my assignment and the responsibility I had to teach these students and the community in general about Africa. I concluded, these students were not only naive, but also too fragile and too gullible.

A few days after this incident, I went to the office of the AFS adviser and discussed with her ways that would enable me to play a greater role in educating my fellow students about Africa and Ghana. We chartered a course of action. We would do two things. We decided that I would start a column in the school newspaper which became known as "Kofi's Column." In this column, I would write about the differences that I had perceived between Africa and America, covering such topics as foods, marriage, customs, school life and educational systems, politics, and the weather.   This, I believed would give me an opportunity to bring Africa to our student body as well as the Albany community in general.   This approach proved much more successful than we had anticipated.   We received letters from many readers who expressed their satisfaction about the topics covered, and talked of the knowledge they had since acquired about Ghana and Africa.   My "peanut butter soup" recipe that was published in the school and Albany newspapers elicited a large response from readers who either wanted more information or were writing to express their delight with the recipe.

Our second plan was to get me out to meet people in the community and to talk more about Africa and Ghana.   I would spend more time than what was ordinarily required under the program, talking to churches, high schools, the Chamber of Commerce, and other social and civic clubs, such as the Kiwanis Club. This approach was equally successful and in fact gave me an opportunity to meet a lot of important and influential people, some of whom eventually helped me to return to America after my year as an exchange student at South Albany.

My major experience with black Americans in the United States did not occur until about halfway through my year at South. I had seen a few blacks in New York City and Corvallis, and had met briefly with a black family in Albany at a grocery store. But I had not had much dealings with these people. But this was all to change, and soon.

I still had not gotten over my African habit of avoiding my teachers and superiors whenever I could, so I usually stayed away from my AFS adviser at South. I seldom ever went to her office voluntarily. Whenever she needed me, she would leave a message for me. And whenever she left a message for me, I always took it seriously, always apprehensive that something must be amiss. So when she left a message for me this time, I did not hesitate to rush to her office to find out what she needed me for. She suggested that my experience in the United States would be incomplete until I had a chance to live in a predominantly black community. And so she had arranged for me to spend a week at Adams High school in Portland, Oregon. She also told me that during my stay in Portland I would live with a black family, the Josephs.

Adams High, being a predominantly black high school, was to be the entry point for my orientation to black America.   That was one of the reasons for its selection. It was also selected because Adams High School was a rather unique experimental school. It was designed as an experimental school that would give students great latitude in making their own decisions with little supervision, direction, or input from teachers. For example, at the time students at Adams could choose to come to school anytime they wanted, leave when they chose, and basically do whatever they pleased while at school. This was really a new world for me.

Having lived most of my life at a boarding school where discipline was strictly enforced and students had little or no say in their own affairs, I felt that

the students at South Albany High already had too much freedom. But at
Adams? It was a whole new ball game! I recall writing in my newspaper
column after I returned from Adams to south, "Adams High School is, rather
than Africa, the real jungle!"

The differences between Adams and South were overwhelming. The students
at Adams, blacks and whites, were incredibly noisy and rowdy, but above all
they had the look of violence about them. They smoked cigarettes and
marijuana even in the hallways, played their music loud, and danced along the
hallways. They looked tough and acted defiantly. Indeed, they were rebellious.
I had never previously seen such student behavior. I thought initially that there
was just no way that I could identify or fit in with these students. They were
just too different for me, and I actually was frightened to walk by whenever they
were gathered together. This was a cultural shock, the greatest one I had
experienced since my arrival in the United States. However, I must add that at
the end of my two-week stay at Adams, I had made quite a few friends and had
begun to understand, albeit quite slowly, why these students behaved the way
they did.

The Josephs were very different from these students. They were a middle-
income and a very loving, stable family. They were as American as they come,
but they also had something African about them. They were quite
knowledgeable about Africa and Ghana. They had asked me to stay with them
to enhance their knowledge of Africa and as I was also told later, to get their
children interested in the continent and thus to encourage them to learn more
about it.

I took to this family very quickly. There was, as I said, something about
them that impressed me most profoundly -- perhaps because they were the first
black family I had met and gotten to know, or simply because they appeared too
successful for what I had expected a black family to be. Before coming to the
United States, I did not know much about American blacks. Most Africans in
Africa tend to associate black Americans with oppression, deprivation, poverty,
and alienation. This family was very different. Perhaps my fascination with the
Josephs could also be due to the poor impression the black students at Adams
had given me about black Americans. In any event, it was very refreshing to
know that all blacks were not like the students I had met at Adams. Perhaps,
for all these reasons, the Josephs were very special to me.

They were as eager to learn about Africa as I was to learn about the United
States, particularly about black America. There were still many questions that
I needed answers for, questions about race and racism, but for fear of
embarrassing my host family (the Robertsons) I had put them on the back
burner. Now there was a real opportunity to discuss these questions, perhaps
with people who might be even more knowledgeable about the issues.

Since my arrival in the United States, I had been wanting to know why blacks
were discriminated against and why they would not leave this country to settle
in Africa if they were so unwanted here. During my two-week stay in Portland,

I had a chance to raise these issues. We talked extensively about race problems in the United States and discussed many issues about Africa that were of interest to the Josephs family. I had insisted that Africans loved blacks in the United States and that we viewed them no less than our brothers and sisters and that they were very welcome to visit, and indeed to move and settle in Africa. Being as naive as I was then, I was even convinced that it was possible for all the blacks in the United States to move back to Africa and adjust quickly to life there.

After this visit, I felt relatively more knowledgeable about blacks and racial issues than before; nevertheless, I still could not explain why there were racial problems in the United States. I suppose that the explanation given to me was so nonsensical that it did not register with my brain. The explanation was that blacks were discriminated against by whites because they were thought to be intellectually inferior to whites. I felt sorry for the predicament of blacks in this country and felt a personal responsibility, as an African, for the part my forebears had played in their tragedy. The emotional attachment to this family had been great. But more importantly, we understood ourselves very clearly. I had come to the United States as an ambassador of goodwill, and therefore I had a responsibility to be open minded about the American society, about whites as well as blacks.

I had sensed that the Josephs somehow felt that the discussions we had could potentially ruin my relationship with the Robertsons. I assured them, however, that I was capable of handling my family relationships in an objective manner and that my affection for the Robertsons had actually intensified, not declined. The Robertsons, like any other white family, could have been prejudiced. However, they have chosen not to be, and not only that, they had accepted me completely as one of them. I said to myself, so why should these discussions adversely affect our relationship? If any, they should help it. I also assured the Josephs that, now more than ever, I was prepared to raise the race issue with them and to seek their views about racism in the United States.

But before this was over, I also had to reassure myself. As if responding to a question, I told them that I had never even had the occasion to view myself as being inferior to a white person. I argued, after all, that I was born in a predominantly black country and that my superiority, or the lack of it, had never being challenged. I argued on -- maybe it was the blacks in this country who were viewed as being inferior to the whites, not us Africans. Inspired by the looks on their faces, I continued: "We Africans are our own boss in our countries. We are a free people, and in spite of our economic and political problems, we do not have any inferiority complex. We will not even entertain the idea, much less accept, that we are inferior because some white person says so!" The anger and the emotion that were evident in my voice as I spoke were so strong that I felt I may have offended them. Indeed, I felt that my response had been too strong for a question nobody had asked.

To the contrary, they were actually impressed with what they called "my positive attitude" and emphasized that that was the only attitude with which I could survive the "racism in the United States." They argued that the whites had been so successful in destroying the black people's self-confidence and self-esteem that many blacks had actually accepted, either consciously or subconsciously, that they were inferior to the whites. Mr. Josephs warned: "Do not become a victim of this! Hold your head high, and you will do well." I assured him that I might be very naive about many things, but if I were convinced of anything at all, it was about my self-esteem and confidence.

The rest of my stay in Portland was full of fun, and I enjoyed every minute of it. When I left two weeks later, Vernon, the eldest son of the family, gave me a present that didn't mean very much to me at first but eventually helped intensify my curiosity and desire to continue to find answers to some of the racial questions that I had raised -- the answers to which raised many more questions in my mind than had been resolved. I needed more satisfactory and convincing answers to the question of racism in the United States than had been offered so far.

The gift Vernon gave to me was a record album by Marvin Gaye, "What's Going On." He had specially given the album to me, as I would find out later, to convey a particular message to me about racism and the plight of blacks in the United States. However, the message was initially lost on me. For at first I could not make out the words clearly and as such could not follow much of the lyrics on the album. As a result, I could not relate the words on the album to the life of black Americans in the United States. Yet, I liked the record and played it over and over again until the words eventually began to make sense to me.

After I returned to Albany, I did not meet any more blacks, and except for one or two occasions that the family talked about race problems in general in the United States, the race issue appeared to have receded into the past -- evidently, not for too long, however. The seeds of curiosity had been sowed. The Josephs had made a great impression on my young and fragile mind, and it was only a matter of time before the fruits would be harvested.

During one of my speaking engagements, I met an official from Oregon State University, Dr. Marvin Durham. Dr. Durham was attending one of the monthly meetings of the Kiwanis Club in Albany. I was the guest speaker for that day. After my speech, he came forward, introduced himself, and congratulated me for my "brilliant performance." He also pointed out to me that he was the foreign student adviser at Oregon State University, and he invited me to visit the school whenever I was in Corvallis. He further indicated to me that there were two Ghanaians attending Oregon State University. He gave their telephone numbers to me and suggested that I contact them since I had not met any Ghanaian for so long. Indeed, I had not met any Ghanaian since I had been in the United States. Obviously, I was very anxious to meet the Ghanaian students at Oregon State University.

About four weeks after meeting Dr. Durham in Albany, I paid a visit to

Oregon State University and met with Dr. Durham again. He was as pleasant as ever. He discussed the programs at the university with me and personally took me on a tour of the campus. I was impressed with the beauty of the campus, the diversity of the university's course offerings, and the sizable number of foreign students enrolled there. After we returned to his office, he asked me if I planned to return to the states after I completed my exchange program. I indicated to him that I was not sure.

One of the requirements of the AFS program was that a participant must return to his country and stay there for at least two years before he could return to the United States. The rationale was that the two-year stay in the student's home country would give him enough time and opportunity to share his experiences in the United States with his friends, school mates, family, and community. To my knowledge, at the time, no one had been able to return to the United States without fulfilling the two-year residency requirements. I also emphasized to him however, that if there was an opportunity to return to the United States, I would be most happy to come to Oregon State University. Without any hesitation, I also made it clear to him that I did not have the money to pay for my education in the States, even if I were offered admission to a university here.

Detecting that perhaps I sounded too negative, he interjected and said, "depending on your grades at South, you could qualify for a scholarship from the State of Oregon." I told him that I had a high (3.88 on a 4.00 scale) grade point average from South Albany and hoped to graduate near the top of my class. He gave me the necessary admission forms, including an application for a State of Oregon scholarship.

In January 1974, six months after my graduation from South Albany, I enrolled as a freshman at Oregon State University. Between the six months of graduation and my enrollment at Oregon State, I spent about two months in Ghana and four months in New York City. I returned from Ghana after graduation from South, following a nationwide tour organized by AFS for all the program participants that year. My determination to return to the United States was only surpassed by my eagerness to find a way to support the trip and the subsequent educational expenses.

During my year in Albany, I had worked on weekends and after school for my host father at his taxidermy shop, where I had made $1 an hour. I had also mowed lawns for the neighbors and had done other chores and menial jobs. As a result I had saved about $600 during the year. When the time came for me to leave for Ghana, I had saved close to $900. Even though I had come to America as an exchange student for only one year, during which time I was legally not allowed to seek employment, I was very much aware of the expectations that awaited me at home. You just don't return from the United States without a lot of gifts for every one in the (extended) family -- not even if you had stayed for only a day. After all, in the United States, the sidewalks are "paved with gold." To meet these expectations, and indirectly helping to perpetuate them, I spent about half of my life's savings on gifts.

When I got to Ghana, I had about $300 left and intended to save this to pay my way back to the United States. Meanwhile, my applications for admission and scholarship at Oregon State had been successful. The scholarship would pay for all my tuition and fees. I was required to pay for my room and board, and this instantly became the new challenge. Where in the world was I going to get this money from?

When all my attempts to raise this money failed in Ghana, I left for the United States, determined this time to find some of the streets that everybody in Ghana told me are "paved with gold." I arrived in New York City in late August with about $100 in my pocket. With this money, I needed no convincing that I could not pay my fare to Oregon, much less pay for room and board at Oregon State. An American family in Ohio that had earlier promised to help me financially reneged on its promise. I was now stranded in New York City. Luckily, I managed to locate a Ghanaian whom I had met in Long Island during the AFS tour a few months before. He agreed to have me stay with him and to help me get a job. This, needless to say, meant that I couldn't enroll at Oregon State in the fall of 1973 as I was expected to do and as part of the conditions for my scholarship.

I put in a phone call to Dr. Durham to explain my situation to him. He was most unhappy about my suggestion of staying in New York for a whole quarter and also to work illegally. He argued that it was against Immigration regulations for me to work without a student work permit, which could not be issued to me even if he wanted to, and that I could be deported if I were caught. He also warned me that my scholarship would be withdrawn if I did not enroll in the fall quarter.

For me, the decision had been made. I simply did not have enough money even to pay my fare to Oregon! I thought this was simple enough. I either had to work to earn additional money or break the bank. I thought the first option was more attractive. Dr. Durham never truly forgave me. I had disappointed him, but he would do all he could to maintain my scholarship until the winter quarter.

Less than a week after my arrival in New York City, I got a job in a factory assembling watches in Chinatown. I made about $80 a week. I worked seven days a week, including holidays. By the end of December, I had saved over $1,000 and was ready to go back to Oregon. I had made just about the right amount of money to pay for the two quarters before the summer vacation, when I hoped I would be able to work again. I could not afford to be wasteful in any way. I needed to get to Oregon by the cheapest possible means. After checking all the available fares, I found that it would cost me about $100 less to go by bus from New York City to Corvallis than by air.

I was also told that the trip would take about five days and nights! In fact, the man at the bus terminal advised me to take the plane since the $100 differential between the two fares was not significant enough to warrant such a long and miserable winter drive. Many of my friends gave me the same advice, but I knew what the additional $100 meant to me and I was not about to take any chances with a cent of that money. Defying all the unsolicited advice, I set off on January 1, 1974, for Oregon, arriving in Corvallis on January 6.

If the blacks at Adams High School had disappointed me, my four month stay in New York City had helped to provide some insights into their behavior. For the first time, I had actually lived among blacks, worked with them, dated some black girls, and had come face to face with the obstacles they had to overcome as the underclass in the United States. I had myself become a victim of discrimination and was convinced that I was no more immune to racism or bigotry than any other black person in the United States. My experience in Harlem had convinced me that black is black, regardless of whether one was from Africa or from the United States. I could now relate to some of their frustrations, the broken dreams and hopes, and, indeed, I had also seen some of the weaknesses and vulnerabilities of blacks in the United States.

Living in the heart of Harlem, I met the real American underclass. I saw and heard more about poverty, crime, drug abuse, murder, rape, and drunkenness in those four months than I had in all my lifetime. I realized then that America had not been the "land of the free" for most of the blacks with whom I had come into contact in Harlem, and met subsequently across the United States.

The rights set forth in the Declaration of American Independence and in the Constitution have become elusive dreams rather than a reality for most of my friends and neighbors in Harlem. Many of the blacks I had met at that time remained outside of American society looking in. They lived in the ghettos, in crowded and substandard housing. Many never went to school, but those who did attended in old schools with standards below those of the white schools. Recently, an article in a United States weekly news magazine characterized life in the ghetto for black kids,

Many drop out or simply succumb to rats, crime, or to drugs. If one is lucky, he may survive the crime, the rats, the drugs and the gangs. He may even graduate from high school and finish college. But his problems will be far from over. He may yet be discriminated against in his job, in promotion, and in housing.

Above all, he may be accepted not because he is deemed competent or as a human being, but because a piece of legislation says he should.

As I traveled more throughout the United States, read and watched more American news, and talked to many more blacks, I found that the problems faced by the blacks whom I had met in Harlem were not peculiar to them but afflicted many other blacks throughout the United States. I also found that, yes, many blacks may have moved into the middle-class status since the passage of the Civil Rights Acts of the 1960s, yet, many now appear stuck to the bottom of the economic ladder, unable to rise through society, but festering at its base.

In 1963 President Kennedy painted a vivid portrait of the life, conditions, and obstacles that faced a black person in this great land of opportunity and freedom. He stated:

The Negro baby born in America today, regardless of the section of the Nation in which he is born, has about one-half as much chance of completing high school as a white baby born in the same place on the same day, one-third as much chance of completing college, one-third as much chance of becoming a professional man, twice as much chance of becoming unemployed, about one-seventh as much chance of earning $10,000 a year, a life expectancy which is 7 years shorter, and the prospects of earning only half as much.[1]

This is a hefty price to pay for being born with black skin in a nation where "all men are created equal." But Kennedy's portrait does not include the daily indignities, humiliations, abuses, rebuffs, and defeats that have become a common feature of the daily life of many blacks in the United States. Although President Kennedy's assessments were the most obvious ones, Ralph Ellison contends that the not-so-obvious features are just as painful. What can be worse than becoming invisible in the society in which you live? But this is exactly how Ellison describes the black adult in the United States: "I am an invisible man." He wrote, "I am a man of substance, of flesh and bone, fiber and liquids -- and I might even be said to possess a mind. I am invisible, understand, simply because people refuse to see me."[2]

Ellison wrote these words in 1947. Today the black man in the United States may not be totally invisible, but that is not to imply that racism no longer exists in the United States, or that white's attitudes toward blacks have fundamentally changed. An important change, however, is that blacks with the help of some white liberals fought to get the civil rights laws passed. For this reason, blacks may now be recognized, not as equal, but at least as being of substance, fresh, and perhaps even as having a brain!

For the black person in the United States, a lot has changed, but much remains the same. The emphasis of the black man's struggle in the United States has now shifted from civil rights to economic rights, from voting rights to political rights. And a lot of the gains have been made in the political sphere. Nevertheless, a lot remains to be done, particularly in the economic realm. I have personally witnessed many changes in political participation and acquisition of political power by blacks in this country since my arrival in the United States in the early 1970s.

In 1970, for example, a total of 1,469 blacks held elective office at all levels of government including ten members of Congress. By 1984, there were 5,600 black elected officials throughout the country and twenty one black members of Congress. Today, four blacks serve in high-level cabinet positions in the Clinton administration, there is a black U.S. senator, and a black serves on the U.S. Supreme Court. There are over 251 black mayors in American cities, and until recently, five black mayors were running the affairs of some of America's largest cities -- New York, Chicago, Los Angeles, Detroit, and Philadelphia.

Black mayors also govern Atlanta, Newark, Washington, D.C., and New Orleans.

On the surface, these gains look very impressive. These significant political gains were achieved in a period of a little over a decade. However, these are only a small part of the total picture. Only slightly more than 1 percent of all elected officials in America today are blacks.

There have been some significant economic gains too. As discussed in Chapter 1, over the past two decades, the size of the black middle class has expanded and grown much faster than the white middle class, with the proportion of blacks making more than $50,000 a year (in 1990 dollars) increasing by 46 percent compared to a 35 percent increase among white families.[3]

Nonetheless, the economic gains for the average black man in the United States remain quite dismal and disappointing. Life in the ghettos may be just as bad today as it was when President Kennedy made his bleak assessment of the life of a black man in the 1960s. For example, Kennedy talked about blacks making less than half of the income of whites then in 1960s. Is it better today?

A Census Bureau Survey reported that median family income for blacks was $14,506 in 1983 compared to $25,757 for whites. Moreover, in 1987, 37.3 percent of all blacks in the United States lived below the poverty line compared to 12.4 percent of all whites.[4] The unemployment rate for blacks was 18.9 percent in 1982 compared to 8.6 percent for whites. For black teenagers, the rate was much higher -- 48 percent in mid-1983 compared to about 12 percent for whites in the same age group. Of the 1.5 million black families headed by a woman, 50 percent live in poverty. For these families, poverty is handed down from generation to generation.[5]

If President Kennedy thought that too many blacks lived in the ghettos in the 1960s, just as many are being born and raised there in the 1990s. Today over 33 percent of all black children are being brought up in poverty compared to 9 percent of white children. Worse yet, many of these children are being brought up in the ghettos of the big cities where "the schools are short of money, housing is vandalized and dilapidated and social services are the poorest." Not surprisingly, 60 percent of black school kids in New York City, as well as many cities across the United States drop out of school.[6] Many are raised in poor environments and in poor company. Many in the company of hardened criminals, drug dealers and pimps -- all poor role models for impressionable young people. In such an environment, violence necessaril, became a permanent feature of their lives. Not suprisingly, black kids do not need to develop a culture of violence, violence becomes the culture.

Many of these black youths, poorly educated, unemployed, alienated and ostracized by society, and raised in a culture of violence, feel naturally bound to commit crime. For these blacks, for whom too many hopes have been frustrated and too many aspirations have been cut short, the natural outlet is commission of crime. To them this is the only way they can hit back at society.

Today the population of the United States' prisons is almost half black (even though blacks constitute only 13 percent of the total U.S. population). Murder is the second highest cause of death among young black men in the sixteen to thirty four age group.[7] In 1983, nearly seven thousand were killed, most of them by other blacks. In 1991, 85 percent of all crimes perpetrated against blacks were committed by blacks. [8] In what has become known as "black on black" crime, blacks are increasingly finding each other an easy target to vent their anger and frustration against society -- they are murdering, raping and robbing each other.

But blacks are not only killing each other, but are also destroying whatever is left of the concept of family in the black community. Today, 68 percent of all black births are out of wedlock, compared to only 22 percent for all whites.[9] While 42 percent of babies born to blacks teenagers were illegitimate in 1960, in 1983 the figure was 89 percent.[10] Nearly half of black females in the United States are pregnant by age 20.[11] In addition, 70 percent of all black families are headed by a woman.[12] A difficult question that must be faced squarely by leaders in the black community if the race is to survive in America is, Are all these problems attributable to racism? In other words, can all the problems of black Americans be explained away by racism?

I am acutely aware of the sensitivity of this question. I do not believe that I have the professional expertise to do full justice to the issue, nor have I done enough research to provide a conclusive answer to the question. But I know that as an African, who was also recently involved in politics in my home country and had to deal with a similar issue, albeit, not any more successfully than black Americans have been able to do with the issue of racism, this is a different question to answer. As an African, I have often been confronted with a similar question: Can all of Africa's economic, social, and political problems be attributed to colonialism?

Many Africans and Westerners alike tend to agree that, yes, Africans' problems are the result of colonialism. For these people, colonialism created the artificial national boundaries that have given rise to the civil wars that we see in Africa today. The result of these civil wars have been the current starvation and massive human suffering that has come to symbolize Africa. Colonialism also eroded the Africans' sense of pride and imposed alien rules, culture, and values as well as cultural imperialism on Africans, while robbing the continent of its natural resources. It is argued that the poverty, the starvation, the heightened tribal sentiment, the political corruption and dictatorship, the political instability, the poor and incompetent management of Africa's natural and human resources, and the cultural alienation that we see today in Africa are the direct result of colonialism.

Although I believe that many of Africa's problems are the direct result of colonialism, and indeed many of those cited above are due to colonialism. I also believe that since most of Africa became independent in the early 1960s, Africans have not demonstrated any great capacity and skill to overcome tribalism, corruption, political dictatorship and intolerance, and inefficient management of their natural and human resources. Africans have not rejected the colonial structures left behind by the colonialist. They have not set up new administrative, political, educational, and economic structures that are needed to deal with the unique problems that faced the postindependent Africa. As I stated in my other book: "African leaders conveniently blame colonialism . . . for all African problems. Yet as successor to the colonial state, they have perpetuated and accentuated the systems, institutions, and structures set up by the colonialist. They blame colonialism while embracing neocolonialism."[13]

When not blaming colonialism, Africans choose to blame an unfair international economic order, demanding that the world economic order be changed before Africa can perform economically. Yes, as an African, I am equally frustrated about the unfair trading and economic system that prevails today in the world. I am also angry that the unfair economic order makes it increasingly difficult for any developing country to emerge from its destined poverty status. But I am also aware that in the same unfair economic system, many countries that have pursued prudent economic policies and have created the right political and business environment have developed economically. In what has recently been referred to as the Asian success stories, countries such as South Korea, Thailand, Taiwan, Indonesia, Malaysia, Hong Kong, and Singapore have done quite well.

Yes, colonialism happened, and we cannot do much to undo it. Of course we cannot forget it, and the world must know that it happened. The world economic order is unfair, but it is not about to be changed any time soon. Even if it were to change soon, we cannot wait for it to change before we start acting to improve our poor and dependent economic status. So where does this leave us? It leaves us with only one solution: Africa must rise above colonialism and the unfair world economic order by pursuing prudent economic policies, taking the necessary actions that can restore internal tranquility and developing the appropriate economic, political, and other institutional structures that can facilitate economic and human development. If Africa could keep its own house clean, it would be stronger and much more united to embark on changing the world economic order. As it is, Africa is too weak economically, politically, and morally to be taken seriously.

In a sense, this is the same attitude with which I approach the race problem in the United States. It seems to me that racism is not about to disappear from the United States, and so black Americans must learn to rise above it. There is pessimism about the future of race relations in the United States. A poll conducted by USA Today/CNN/ Gallup released on August 27, 1993, found that about half of all blacks and a third of whites, now see the United States as moving "towards two societies -- one black, one white, separate and unequal." While in 1963 just 20 percent of blacks said relations between blacks and whites will "always be a problem," in this poll 52 percent blacks had that opinion.

Racism notwithstanding, blacks cannot wait for whites to change before they begin to live their lives in dignity and achieve economic prosperity. The American blacks, like the Africans, must learn to do for themselves what whites cannot do for them -- they must learn to like themselves, care about each other, and work together for a change. After all, the black teenagers having illegitimate babies are not having them with white folks. While the whites may be supplying the drugs, they are peddled in the ghettos by blacks themselves.

The black-on-black killings which have become so common in the United States today, like African dictators killing millions of their own people, cannot always be blamed on white people. Some see the problems of blacks as part of a grand conspiracy of white people to destroy the black race. Even if this were true, as many blacks believe, should blacks be such eager and willing partners in their self-annihilation?

It seems to me that blacks cannot forever continue to accuse the "devil" for making them do all the bad things they do. In the same environment of racism, many recent immigrants to the United States are making it, just as many Asian countries are making it in the same unjust and unfair international economic order. Perhaps American blacks, like Africans need to overcome the feeling that somehow the world owes them something, and rather should go out there and strive to do things for themselves. Nearly two decades ago, in 1964, Malcolm X declared:

The social philosophy of black nationalism only means that we have to get together and remove the evils, the vices, alcoholism, drug addiction, and other evils that are destroying the moral fiber of our community. We ourselves have to lift the level of our community, the standard of our community to a higher level, make our society beautiful so that we will be satisfied in our social circle. *So it is not necessary to change the white man's mind. We've got to change our own minds about each other*[14] (emphasis mine).

Nonetheless, I see the problems faced by blacks in this country as problems for all Americans, not just black Americans. It is more of a moral dilemma that strikes at nothing less than the basic foundations of this country -- freedom, equality, and the pursuit of happiness. The United States cannot claim to be a free nation with some of its citizens living in freedom and others living in economic and social bondage. It cannot claim to be a free nation until all its citizens are free. President Kennedy echoed this sentiment in 1963, "And this nation, for all its hopes and in all its boasts, will not be fully free until all its citizens are free."[15] Blacks in the United States, Charles Silberman notes, are "an economic as well as a racial minority." He argues, no matter how "acculturated" the black American becomes, because of his skin color, "he can not lose himself in a crowd. He remains a Negro . . . an alien in his own land."[16]

Yes, the black man may still be an alien in his own land, but the question is for how long? "We shall have our manhood. We shall have it or the earth will be levelled by our attempts," said Eldridge Cleaver. For Malcolm X, it was, either the ballot or the bullet." But these were the sentiments of the 1960s. In the 1990s, the black man is still trying to win his manhood, except that now he wants to do so through the attainment of economic and political power. "There is a freedom train coming, but you have to register to ride it," exalts Reverend Jesse Jackson.[17]

For many blacks in the United States, one of their proudest moments came in 1983 Jesse Jackson declared his candidacy for the Democratic party's presidential nomination. For many, it was more symbolic than anything: his candidacy was a rejection by the black American of the second-class status that the whites had conferred on him. It was an upliftment of the spirit of the black man. As Jackson himself declared, it was "a move from the outhouse to the courthouse, guttermost to the uppermost, slaveship to the championship, Statehouse to the Whitehouse."[18] But above all, Jackson's candidacy was the ultimate embodiment of the American political ideal, an affirmation that every child of the United States, yes, even the grandchild of a slave, can some day seek the presidency. But this may have been too much to expect of America so soon!

Many whites to whom the thought of a black president was completely unacceptable and others who genuinely did not want Jackson to succeed went to work immediately. "They scrutinized all his actions, gestures, activities, finances, lifestyle and habits. They found nothing to discredit him. They scrutinized his calls for racial pride among blacks, looking for overt signs of racism. But found none."[19] But finally, in a light mood and in an unguarded moment, Jackson made offensive remarks against the Jews.[20] In a matter of days, it set off a chain of events that for all practical purposes destroyed his campaign. As Dan Rather later stated for CBS News, Jackson's run had set off a "white backlash." His candidacy helped ignite old racial prejudices and increased white supremacy sentiments in the United States.

As Hodding Carter, a former official in the Carter administration, would also say later; "We ought to thank Mr. Jackson for running. Not because he should or shouldn't be President, but because his candidacy has helped to put race and things racial back in public view where they belong."[21] Whatever happened thereafter, one thing was clear: the myth or the taboo that a black person could not make a serious ran for the presidency of the United States had been broken. As Jackson himself said, "Whether I win or lose, American politics will never be the same."[22] The USA Today/CNN/Gallup poll cited above reports that whereas in 1960 only 45 percent of whites said they would vote for a "well-qualified" black running for president, today 55 percent of whites say a black would be president in about twenty years.

During my stay in the United States, I have had to answer many questions for both blacks and whites. I have had to explain African culture, life-styles, and food practically everywhere I go. However, two questions have persistently come up. These questions have often been raised by both blacks and whites, and so I would like to address both of them as closing remarks of this chapter.

One of the questions has been, "In what ways is the African different from the Black American?" My answer has always been the same. I have always argued that basically, there are no inherent differences between the two. The perceived differences between us today are due in large part to our different upbringing. Most African students who come to the United States are free and the black Americans are largely not. It is true that African countries may be underdeveloped economically and that they still have enormous economic and political problems. Nevertheless, Africans are a free people. They are free from white domination and alienation. Malcolm X acknowledged this when he said: "In fact, you'd get further calling yourself African instead of Negro . . . . They do not have to pass civil rights bills for Africans. An African can go anywhere he wants right now."[23]

I, for example, was raised in a free country. I have never had to feel sorry for, or apologize for the color of my skin. I have never, before coming to the United States, been treated as an inferior person or as a minority. My self-esteem had never previously been challenged. Above all, my right as a human being, created in the likeness of God, is not granted to me because some piece of legislation was successfully passed, however reluctantly. I have all the rights that any human being in my country can lay claim to because I am a human being.

Obviously, the acculturation processes and the experiences that black Americans have gone through in the United States account significantly for the perceived differences between them and Africans. These experiences may have shaped the differences in perceptions and attitudes between the two groups. For example, the black American has been enslaved, oppressed, humiliated, and abused. As a result of these experiences, their very nature may have changed.

The black American may be perceived by some whites as violent and impatient. But that may be because too many dreams and hopes have been broken. Martin Luther King, Jr., responded to the allegation that blacks were impatient when he said:

We have waited for 340 years for our constitutional and God-given rights . . . Perhaps it is easy for those who have never felt the stinging darts of segregation to say, "Wait." But when you have seen the mobs lynch your mothers and fathers at will and drown your sister and brothers at whim;. . . when you see the vast majority of your twenty million Negro brothers smothering in an airtight cage of poverty in the midst of an affluent society . . . I hope, sirs, you can understand our legitimate and unavoidable impatience.[24]

Perhaps some of the black American traits, such as impatience that the whites see as negative were necessary and perhaps continued to be essential traits for the survival of the black race in the United States during the enslavement and the subsequent racist period.

Again, American blacks may have low self-esteem and low self-confidence, but that was exactly what the white man wanted to do to him all the time. Thus the black man's manhood may have been challenged, and he may have lost some of it, but through all this, he has largely not lost his African personality.

In spite of the common ancestral heritage shared between Africans in the United States and black Americans, the two kindred groups have not always had a harmonious relationship. While Kwame Nkrumah, the late president of Ghana, for example, recalled positive experiences with black Americans during his student days at Lincoln University in Pennsylvania, other Africans have reported some negative experiences with the black community in the United States.

Harlod R. Isaacs' experience with blacks in the United States led him to conclude that Africans who come to the United States were "looked upon as barbarians or ex-barbarians who had become snobbish Europeans. At Negro schools, they were made to feel this prejudice most explicitly and painfully; they were isolated, made the butt of harsh jokes."[25] A study of African students in the United States in 1960, even at the peak of the pan-African movement, concluded that one out of five African students "even in predominantly Negro colleges in the South had no black American friend."[26]

Studies show that some black Americans resent Africans in the United States because these Africans have not identified closely with their cause and have not tried to understand them. Many black Americans feel that the Africans tend to express an air of superiority over them.[27] Others also argue that the hostility between the two kindred groups has been deliberately orchestrated by whites to keep the two groups apart.[28]

I believe that there is an element of truth in each of these three allegations. It seems to me that African students tend not to understand black Americans most of the time. This is due in part to their different backgrounds. First, most African students who come to the United States for the first time have not been subjected to racism in their own countries. As a result, they generally do not have preconceived notions about racism. In other words, they tend to be more open minded about racism and are inclined to deal with blacks and whites on the basis of their character rather than their race. The inability or unwillingness of many Africans to automatically support the black cause has thus been interpreted as lack of concern, understanding, or empathy for the black cause.

The attitude of African students tends to change as they graduate from the university and begin a professional career in the United States. Having been sheltered from racism during their student days in the academic environment, they soon discover the real America. Soon they understand what the black American has been fighting for and why the black Americans act the way they do.

The second question is related to the first. The other question asks whether Africans who come to the United States are treated any better than black Americans. Some have suggested that Africans have tended to fare better than black Americans when it comes to discrimination. My own experiences have led me to conclude that this may not be true in general and that, in fact, the African is more likely to be abused and discriminated against than the black American. A study of African students conducted in 1960 reported that 31 percent of the sample thought they were receiving worse treatment than "American Negroes."[29]

This is simple to explain. When most Africans come to the United States, they are prepared to make a lot of adjustments and to accept some basic facts. Many of them accept the fact that they are here only as visitors and that their stay in the United States is only temporary. Most of the time, even if they know their rights, Africans choose not to assert them. They do not fuss over trivialities. Their self-esteem is rather high. They may not fight to convince anybody that they are not inferior, but they do not accept the notion that they are inferior to anybody.

They are less aggressive and perhaps less emotional than black Americans. Meanwhile, most of them are acutely aware of the poor economic and social conditions that they left behind in Africa. They invariably know who they are, where they are going, and, many times, how to get there. In any event, many Africans also despise the conditions that they left behind in Africa and are determined to make the most of their stay in the United States. When you add up all of the above, you invariably come up with highly motivated and very hard-working African men and women who do not complain very much and do not assert their rights as they should. They are easy to work with and many times easy to be abused.

At school, the Africans are generally quite realistic in their expectations. They are quite aware that they may well be the target of racism and discrimination. Thus, they may have accepted the notion that they can only get a B grade when they clearly should have gotten an A. They are most likely to understand that in order to get an A they may have to get an A plus. But they remain undeterred. They work hard, and soon superiors who earlier on may have been cold towards them begin to warm up to them. Meanwhile, it may have been assumed that they need the education to return to some African country to help their "poor and underdeveloped country." To these Americans, it is a noble gesture to help the poor African who can someday go back to his country to help civilize his people. For this reason, many Americans tend to show some sympathy toward the African student. It may have also been rationalized that the African may even remember this help someday and may become pro-American if he should become an important public figure in his country.

In time, the African student graduates from college and get a job. The poor African who needed help so that he could go home and help his poor impoverished people is now determined to settle in the United States. He is no longer the helpless African but a real economic threat. He wants a job in this country and indeed a piece of the American dream. He may even decide to marry a white woman, buy a house in a white neighborhood, and move into the mainstream American life. Now the ballgame changes completely. The African has changed the rules of the game. This was not supposed to happen. He is no longer the poor African; he is indeed a black man and must be treated accordingly.

Having been sheltered in the relatively liberal academic community and sometimes living with or even supported in various ways by an American family, the African now moves into "the real America." His problems begin. He faces the same problems that his black American counterpart faces in the United States. Some of his professional colleagues will even say that he owes his position to some affirmative action program. Thus he is otherwise unqualified for his position, even when they know very well that he is just as qualified as any of them. He has to constantly prove himself, sometimes to others who are either less qualified or less competent than him. Most promotions are beyond his reach mainly because, they argue, he is not an American citizen. And if he happens to be an American citizen, it would still be argued that "he has an accent and can't be entrusted with major responsibilities." Meanwhile, other foreigners with accents, sometimes much worse than the African, are offered positions that an African would never be offered.

Therefore, my answer to the above question has always been, when it comes to racism in the United States, a real racist makes no distinction between black Africans, black Americans, or black Caribbean. To the racist, black is black, whether made in Africa, America, or the Caribbean!

NOTES

1. John F. Kennedy, "A Moral Imperative," *Vital Speeches of the Day*, 29, No. 18, July 1, 1963, p. 546. Delivered over television and radio, Washington, D.C., June 1963.

2. Ralph Ellison, *The Invisible Man* (New York: Random House, 1947) p. 3.

3. *The Economist*, July 10, 1993, p. 17.

4. Carrell Peterson Horton and Jessie Carney Smith, eds., *Statistical Record of Black America* (Detroit: Gale Research, 1990), p. 267

5. Pete Hamil, "The Underclass is the Most Dangerous Fact of Life in the United States," *Esquire*, March 1988. Reprinted in Mark West, ed., *The Future and Individual* (Acton, Mass.: Copley Publishing Group, 1990) p. 231 p. 231

6. Ibid.

7. Ibid.

8. U.S. Department of Justice, *Source Book of Criminal Justice Statistics 1992* (Washington, D.C.: U.S. Government Printing Office, 1992), p. 289.

9. *Wall Street Journal,* October 29, 1993, p. A14.

10. Hamil, p. 231.

11. *Time*, December 9, 1984, pp. 79-80.

12. Hamil, p. 231.

13. Kofi K. Apraku, *African Emigres in the United States: A Missing Link in Africa's Social and Economic Development* (New York: Praeger Publishers, 1991), p. xv.

14. George Breitman, ed. *Malcolm X Speaks -- Selected Speeches and Statements* (New York: Grove Press, 1966), p. 31. This speech entitled "The Ballot or the Bullet," was delivered in Cleveland, Ohio, in April 1964.

15. Kennedy, "A Moral Imperative," p. 547.

16. Charles E. Silberman, *Crisis in Black and White* (New York: Random House, 1964), pp. 41, 43.

17. *Time*, May 7, 1984 p. 30.

18. *Time*, May 7, 1984 pp. 30-31.

19. For Jackson's "Hymie" remarks against the Jews, see *Time*, May 7, 1984 p. 32.

20. *Time*, May 7, 1984, p. 30.

21. Ibid., p. 32.

22. Breitman, *Malcom X Speaks,* p. 36.

23. Martin Luther King, Jr., "Letter from Birmingham Jail," Reprinted in Mark West, ed., *The Asheville Reader: The Future and the Individual* (Acton, Mass.: Copley Group, 1992), pp. 67 - 68.

24. Harlod R. Isaacs, "A Reporter at Large -- Back to Africa," *The New Yorker,* May 1961, p. 135.

25. Robert G. Weisbord, *Ebony Kinship* (Westport, Conn.: Greenwood Press, 1973), p. 167.

26. Ibid.

27. Ibid., p. 168.

28. Ibid., p. 167. Author is not aware of more recent data on topic.

Selected Bibliography

Apraku, Kofi K. *African Emigres in the United States: A Missing Link in Africa's Social and Economic Development*. New York: Praeger Publishers, 1991.

Asher, Herbert. *Presidential Elections and American Politics: Voters, Candidates, and Campaigns since 1952*. Homewood, Ill.: Dorsey Press, 1976.

Beasley, Joseph. *The Betrayal of Health*. New York: Random House, 1991.

Bennett, W. Lance. *The Governing Crisis*. New York: St. Martin's Press, 1992.

Berman, Ronald et al., eds. *Solzhenitsyn at Harvard*. Washington, D.C., Ethics and Public Policy Center, 1980.

Boahen, Adu A. *African Perspectives on Colonialism*. Baltimore: Johns Hopkins University Press, 1987.

Boorstin, Daniel J. *The Image*. New York: Harper & Row, 1961.

Burkett, Larry. *Whatever Happened to the American Dream*. Chicago: Moody Press, 1993.

Campbell, Angus et al. *The American Voter*. New York: John Wiley & Sons, 1964. (2nd edition)

Dahl, Robert A. *Dilemmas of Pluralist Democracy*. New Haven, Conn. Yale University Press, 1982.

Davidson, Basil. *The Africans*. London: Longmans, Green & Co., Ltd. 1969.

Downs, Anthony. *An Economic Theory of Democracy*. New York: Harper & Row, 1957.

Edelman, Murray. *The Symbolic Uses of Politics*. Chicago: University of Illinois Press, 1970.

Ellison, Ralph. *The Invisible Man*. New York: Random House, 1947.

Flanigan, William H. *Political Behavior of the American Electorate*. Boston: Allyn & Bacon, 1968.

Garraty, John A. *The American Nation*. New York: Harper & Row, 1983.

Ginsberg, Benjamin. *The Consequences of Consent: Elections, Citizen Control and Popular Acquiescence*. Reading, Mass.: Addison-Wesley Publishing Co., 1982.

Karnow, Stanley. *Vietnam: A History*. New York: Viking Press, 1983.

Lamb, David. *The Africans*. New York: Random House, 1982.

Litcher, Robert S., et al. *The Video Campaign*. Washington, D.C.:American Enterprise Institute for Public Policy Research, 1988.

Locke, Don C. *Increasing Multicultural Understanding*. Newbury Park,

Calif.: Sage Publications, Inc., 1992.

Lodge, Henry Cabot. ed. *The Federalist*. New York: Knickerbocker Press, 1895.

McKenna, George, and Stanley Feingold, eds. *Taking Sides*. Guilford, Conn.: The Dushkin Publishing Group, 1993.

Mattabane, Mark. *Kaffir Boy in America*. New York: Charles Scribner's Sons, 1989.

Page, Benjamin I. *Choices and Echoes in Presidential Elections*. Chicago: University of Chicago Press, 1978.

Patterson, Thomas E. *The Mass Media Election*. New York: Praeger Publishers, 1980.

Postman, Neil. *Amusing Ourselves to Death*. New York: Penguin Books, 1986.

Schumpeter, Joseph. *Capitalism, Socialism and Democracy*. New York: Harper Bros., 1947.

Weisbord, Robert G. *Ebony Kinship*. Westport, Conn.: Greenwood Press, 1973.

Index

About the Author

KOFI K. APRAKU, formerly an Assistant Professor of Economics at the University of North Carolina at Asheville, is originally from Ghana. He is the author of *African Emigres in the United States* (Praeger, 1991).

ISBN 0-275-94207-4

EAN

9 780275 942076

90000>

HARDCOVER BAR CODE